REPTILES AND AMPHIBIANS DICTIONARY

An A to Z of cold-blooded creatures

Cupcake is an imprint of Alligator Books Ltd
Gadd House, Arcadia Avenue
London N3 2JU

Printed in China. 10889

Information Icons
Throughout this dictionary, there are special icons next to each entry. These give you more information about each horse.

Globes
These show you where each creature can be found in the world. Small red dots on the globes show where each creature is found in the world.

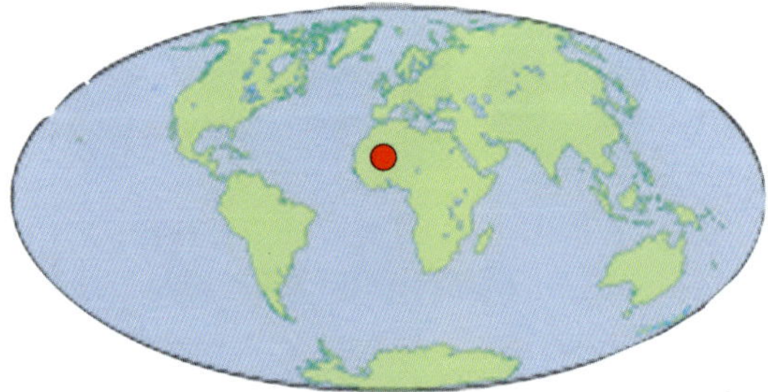

Size Comparison Pictures
Next to each entry is a symbol, either a hand or a man showing the size of each creature in real life.

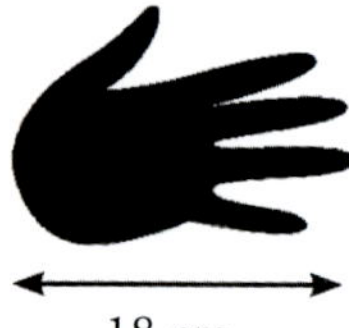

The first symbol is a human adult's hand, which measures about 18 cm (7 inches) from the wrist to the tip of the longest finger. This symbol shows the size of the smaller creatures.

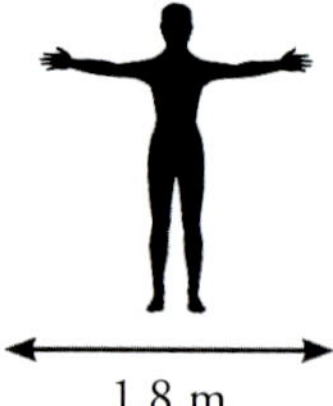

The second symbol is an adult human. With his arms outstretched, his armspan measures about 1.8 m (6 feet). The symbol shows the size of the larger creatures.

REPTILES AND AMPHIBIANS DICTIONARY

An A to Z of cold-blooded creatures

Cold-blooded Life

Red-eyed tree frog

Reptiles and amphibians are part of the animal kingdom known as vertebrates (animals with backbones). All reptiles and amphibians are cold-blooded – their bodies do not produce heat so they rely on the environment for warmth. Mammals and birds are warm-blooded, and their bodies produce heat. There are about 8,000 reptile species and about 5,000 species of amphibian.

Amphibians

An amphibian's body is covered with skin that is rough and 'warty', or smooth and slimy. Amphibians lay soft, jelly-covered eggs. When the eggs hatch, the young begin a juvenile stage, which later develops into an adult stage. Some amphibians spend their whole lives in water, but most spend some time on land when they are adults. Amphibians are divided into two main groups: frogs and toads; and newts and salamanders. Another group is the worm-like caecilians.

Eastern newt

Reptiles

Reptiles have skin that is protected by tough scales. They are completely adapted to life on land. Most reptiles lay eggs, but some lizards and snakes give birth to live young.

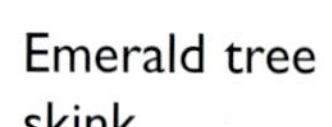
Emerald tree skink

The reptile groups are: tortoises and turtles; lizards; snakes; amphisbaenians; tuatara; and crocodiles and alligators. Most reptiles live on land but some, such as sea turtles, live their entire lives in water. Sea turtles do, however, return to land to lay their eggs.

Yellow-blotched map turtle

Habitats

Being cold-blooded means that reptiles and amphibians rely on the sun and their surroundings to keep their bodies warm. They are most numerous in hot climates. In colder climates, they often hibernate to escape the winter cold. Amphibians spend part of their lives in water, and most return to water in order to lay eggs. They don't go too far from ponds or rivers. Reptiles do well in hot, dry climates. There are many different desert lizards and tortoises.

Black mamba

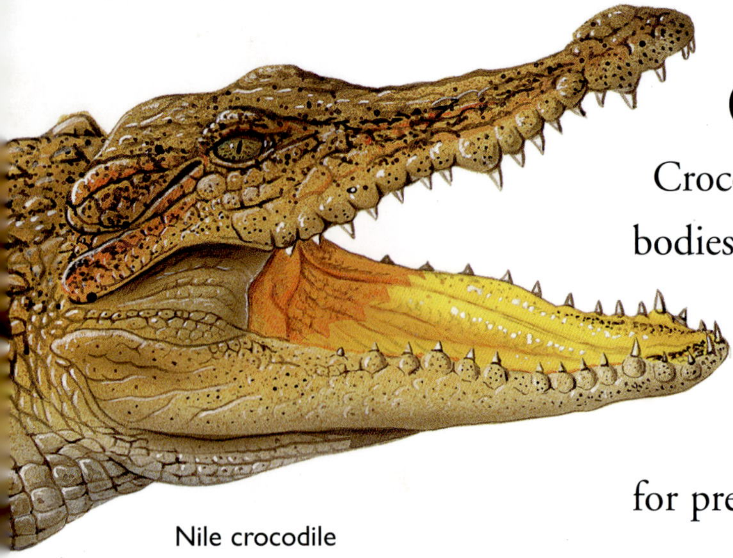

Crocodiles and alligators

Crocodiles and alligators are large reptiles with long bodies and four short legs. They live near water and are excellent swimmers. The skin of crocodiles and alligators is covered with hard, bony plates called scutes. These reptiles are meat-eaters and often hunt for prey on land as well as in the water.

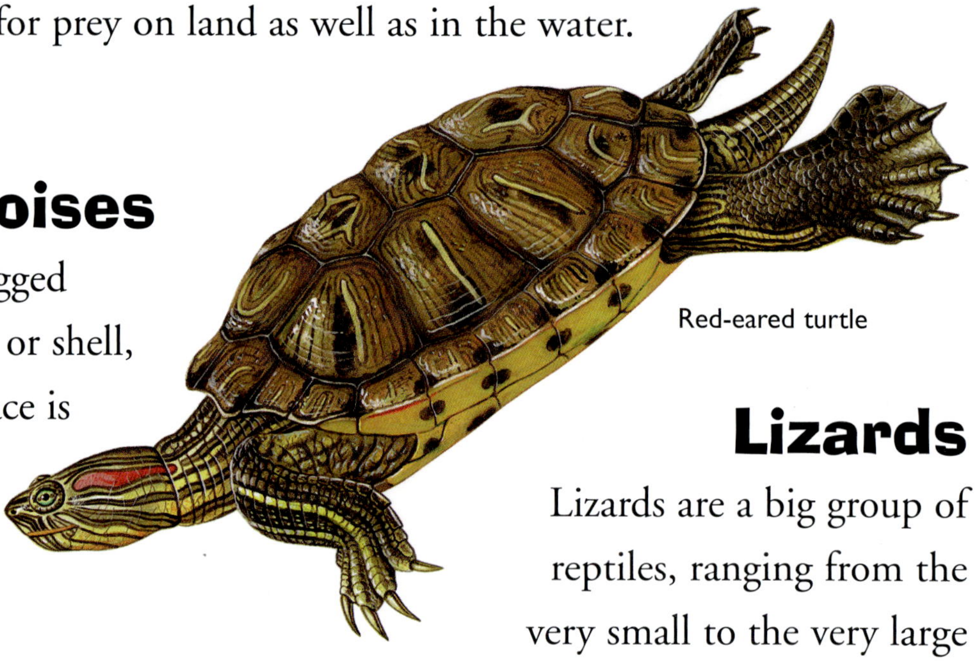

Nile crocodile

Turtles and tortoises

Turtles and tortoises are four-legged reptiles with a domed carapace, or shell, protecting the body. The carapace is usually made of hard plates fused together into a rigid shell. Tortoises live on land, while most turtles live in or near water. Freshwater turtles spend long periods out of the water, sunning themselves. Sea turtles, such as the hawksbill, live their entire lives swimming in the ocean.

Red-eared turtle

Lizards

Lizards are a big group of reptiles, ranging from the very small to the very large Komodo dragon. Most lizards have four legs but some species have only two back legs, or no legs at all. Lizard skin is covered with scales. These are usually small and round, but some lizards have big, spiny scutes that are more like a crocodile's.

Granite night lizard

Snakes

Snakes are legless, mostly meat-eating reptiles. They vary in length from 10 cm (4 inches) to 10 m (33 feet), and are covered with small scales. Snakes are found in most habitats. Some snakes, such as boas and pythons, kill by constriction – they squeeze their victim so that it cannot breathe. Other snakes use sharp fangs to inject venom. Some snakes' venom is strong enough to kill an adult human.

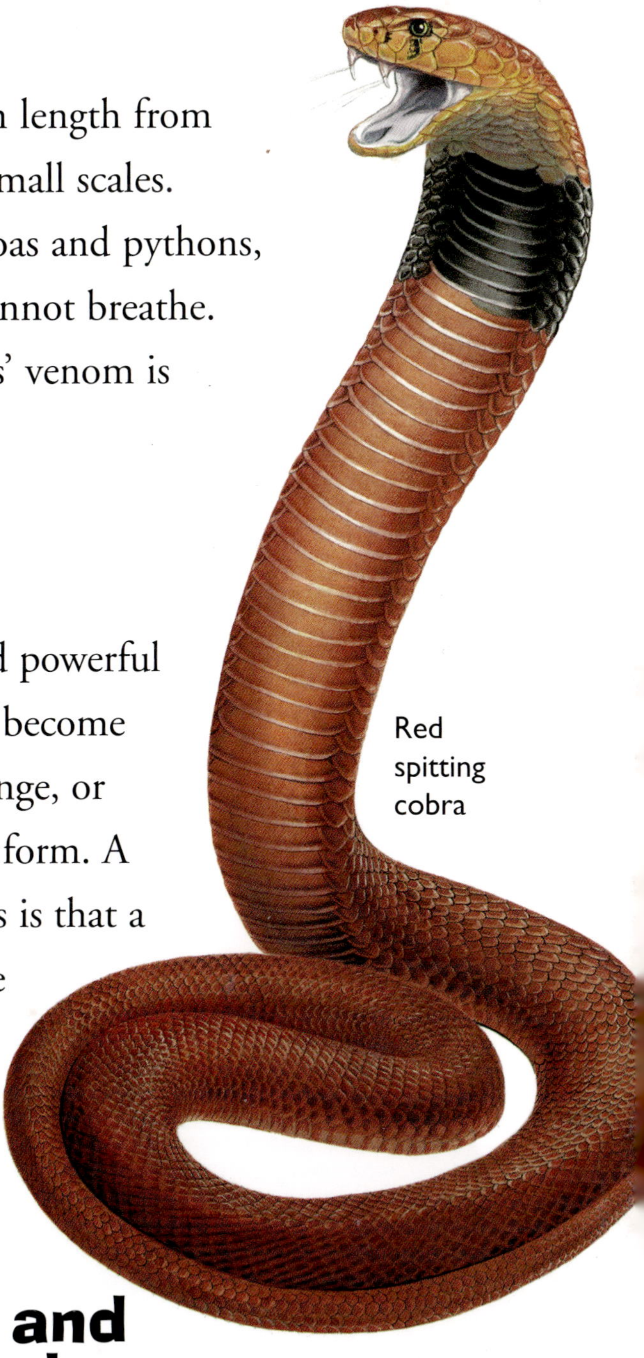

Red spitting cobra

Frogs and toads

Frogs and toads are amphibians with large eyes, no tail, and powerful back legs. The eggs hatch in water to become tadpoles, which undergo a change, or metamorphosis, into the adult form. A difference between frogs and toads is that a toad usually has bumpy skin, while a frog's skin is smooth. Toads also tend to be slower-moving. In tropical regions, many frogs live in trees.

Fire-bellied toad

Slimy salamander

Newts and salamanders

Newts and salamanders are amphibians that usually have four legs and a long tail, but some have only two front legs. Some salamanders spend their entire lives in water, while others live on land as adults. Newts tend to be smaller than salamanders. Some newts live in water all the time, others only when breeding.

Anaconda

The anaconda is the world's heaviest snake, and can grow to up to 9 m (30 feet) in length. The anaconda is a constrictor – it uses its powerful body to prevent its prey from breathing. An adult anaconda can drag its prey underwater to drown it.

Fact

The anaconda does most of its hunting (and resting) in rivers and flooded swamps, because being in water helps support its great weight.

Max length: 18 cm (7 inches)
Amphibian

Arboreal salamander

The arboreal salamander is a small amphibian about 18 cm (7 inches) long, that is found only in the coastal forests of California. Its feet and tail are adapted for tree climbing and it hunts among the branches for insects. It is most active during or after rain. In dry weather, it retreats to an underground burrow.

Armadillo lizard

The armadillo lizard is a desert reptile from southern Africa. Its body is protected by strong, overlapping spines and scales. When it is threatened, the armadillo lizard curls its body into a circle and holds its tail in its mouth. Its body becomes a ring of spines that protects its soft underbelly from predators.

Axolotl

The axolotl is a strange amphibian whose body does not change from its juvenile shape. Instead of losing its juvenile gills and developing lungs like other amphibians, the axolotl keeps its gills during adulthood and spends its whole life in water. Wild axolotls are found only in Lake Xochimilco in central Mexico. This amphibian can regrow a lost limb.

Banded gecko

The banded gecko is a small desert lizard that spends most of the day hiding beneath rocks. It comes out at night to hunt insects and spiders. When the banded gecko is threatened by a predator, it curls its tail over its head to make itself look like a scorpion. If it is caught by its tail, the tail detaches and the gecko grows a new one.

Fact

Some geckos can climb on almost any surface – even upside down. The banded gecko is often found on the underside of rocks.

Bearded dragon

The bearded dragon is a heavy-bodied lizard that lives in the dry forests, scrub and semi-desert of Australia. It feeds mainly on vegetation and insects. It gets its name from its 'beard', which is a jaw pouch of scales. The bearded dragon uses this beard to frighten predators such as snakes and birds of prey.

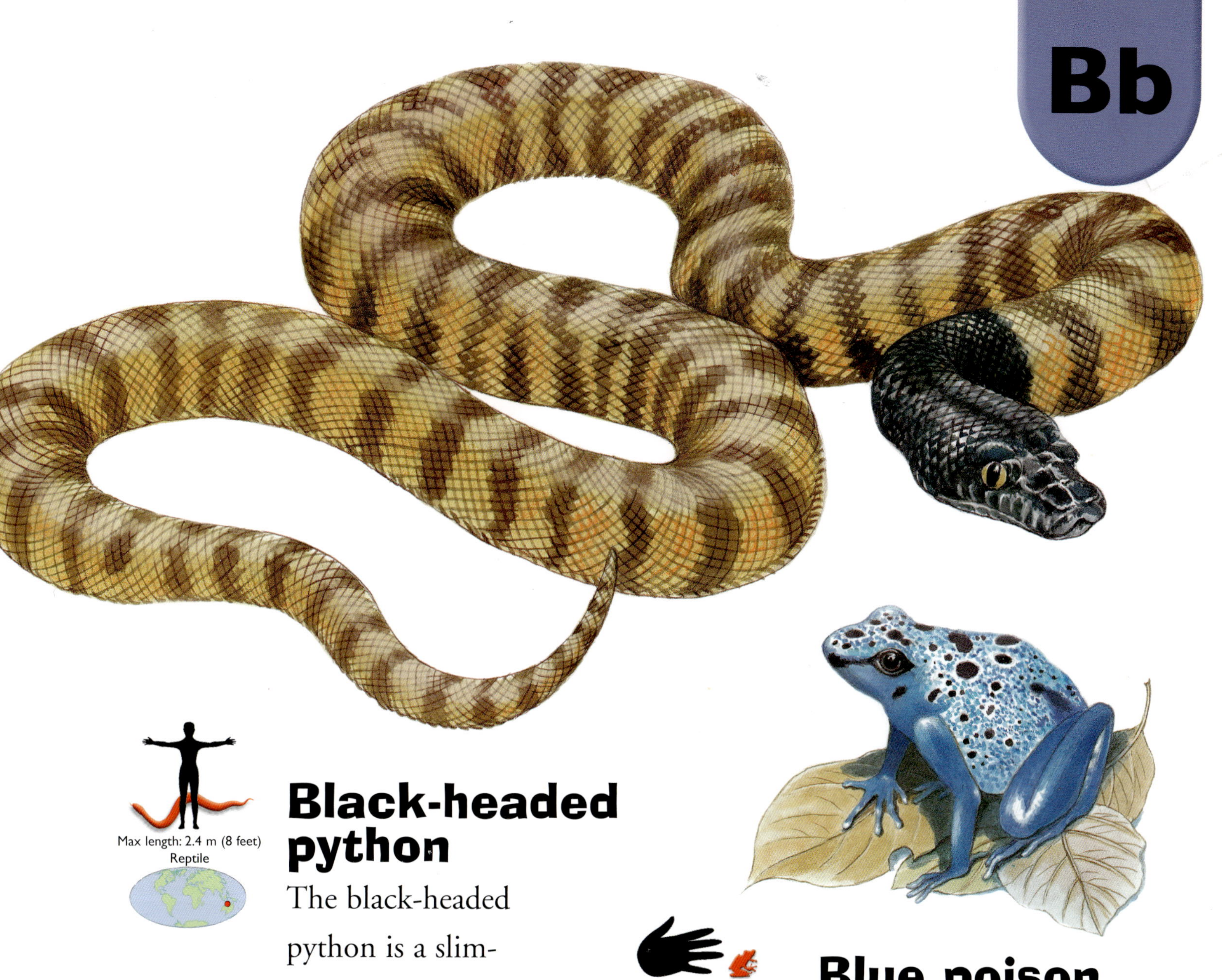

Max length: 2.4 m (8 feet)
Reptile

Black-headed python

The black-headed python is a slim-bodied snake that can grow to more than 2.4 m (8 feet) in length. It lives in northern Australia, where it feeds on small lizards and other snakes. The black-headed python is not venomous – it kills its victims by constriction.

Max length 5 cm (2 inches)
Amphibian

Blue poison dart frog

The blue poison dart frog does not need camouflage to keep it safe from predators in the tropical forests of Central America. The frog's skin produces chemicals that are highly poisonous, and the animal's bright colouration is a warning signal.

Blue-tongued skink

The blue-tongued skink is a medium-sized reptile from eastern Australia. It eats a wide variety of food, including snails, insects, fruit and leaves. The blue-tongued skink has no teeth to defend itself from predators. Instead, it shoots out its large, blue tongue and hisses to frighten away any attackers.

Fact

Although the blue-tongued skink has no teeth, it has powerful jaws and can give a person a painful bite.

Broadley's flat lizard

Broadley's flat lizard is only found on rocks around waterfalls in southwestern Africa, where it feeds on fruit and insects. Sometimes, it leaps into the air to catch flies in its mouth. The lizard's unusually flat body enables it to hide from birds of prey in narrow cracks in the rocks.

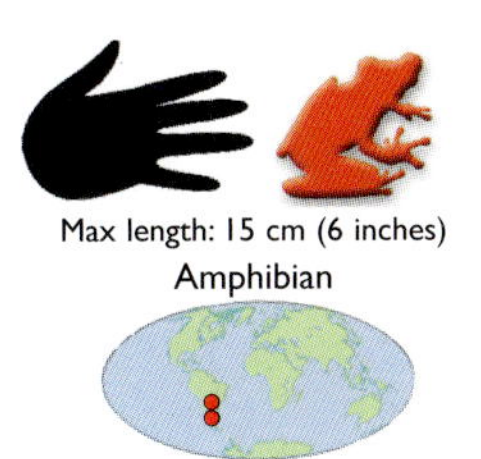

Budgett's frog

Budgett's frog is a strange-looking amphibian from Argentina. It is camouflaged to look like a smooth river pebble. When threatened, Budgett's frog opens its huge mouth and screams and grunts loudly. This aggressive display is enough to frighten away most predators. Those that do not run away are likely to be bitten by this fierce frog.

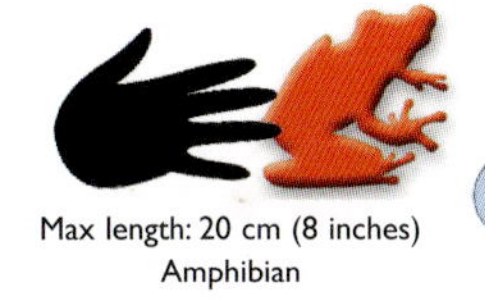

Bullfrog (North American)

The North American bullfrog is the biggest frog in North America, with a body length of up to 20 cm (8 inches). It is an aggressive predator that hunts small mammals and snakes, as well as other amphibians. The pattern on the back of the North American bullfrog varies from region to region, but in some regions it is simply green.

Caiman (black)

The black caiman is a large South American crocodile that can grow to 6 m (20 feet) in length. It feeds mainly on fish and rodents. Juveniles are yellow in colour, but adults are a dull to olive green. The black caiman has been hunted almost to extinction for its skin.

Caiman lizard

The brightly coloured caiman lizard lives near lakes and streams in the tropical forests of South America. It feeds mainly on snails, clams and crayfish that it catches by diving under water. When it is swimming at the surface, it looks like a miniature caiman – so it was named the caiman lizard.

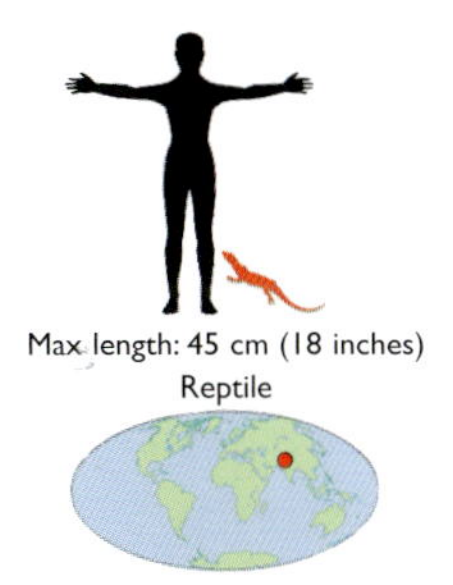

Chinese crocodile lizard

The Chinese crocodile lizard is a rare reptile from the mountain ponds and streams of southern China. It has a ridge of bony scales along its back and tail like a crocodile. If it senses danger, the Chinese crocodile lizard stops in mid-stride and remains motionless, on land or underwater, for several hours.

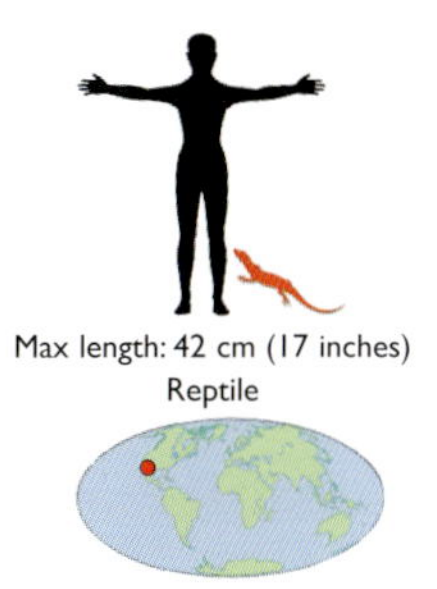

Chuckwalla

The chuckwalla is a medium-sized desert lizard that grows to about 42 cm (17 inches) in length. It feeds on cacti and other vegetation and is active only during the hottest part of the day. When threatened by a predator, the chuckwalla hides in a rock crevice and inflates its body – jammed inside the crevice, it is difficult to pull out.

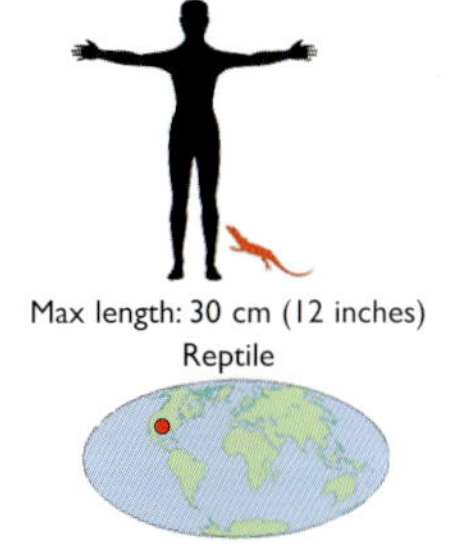

Collared lizard

The collared lizard is a fast-moving desert predator that hunts insects and other lizards during the heat of the day. It is about 30 cm (12 inches) long when full-grown. When escaping from danger, the collared lizard lifts its front legs off the ground and uses its powerful hind legs to run away.

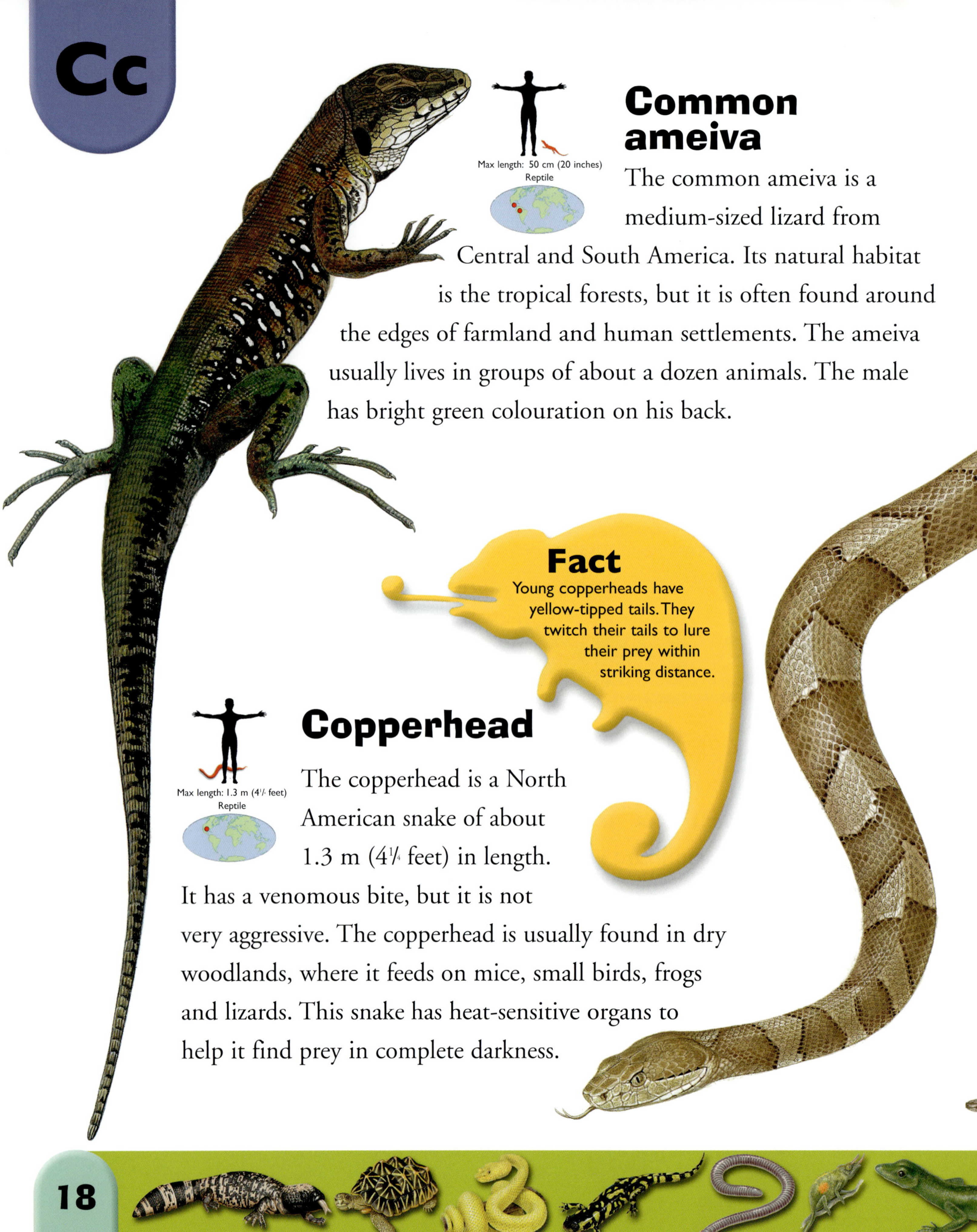

Common ameiva

The common ameiva is a medium-sized lizard from Central and South America. Its natural habitat is the tropical forests, but it is often found around the edges of farmland and human settlements. The ameiva usually lives in groups of about a dozen animals. The male has bright green colouration on his back.

Fact

Young copperheads have yellow-tipped tails. They twitch their tails to lure their prey within striking distance.

Copperhead

The copperhead is a North American snake of about 1.3 m (4¼ feet) in length. It has a venomous bite, but it is not very aggressive. The copperhead is usually found in dry woodlands, where it feeds on mice, small birds, frogs and lizards. This snake has heat-sensitive organs to help it find prey in complete darkness.

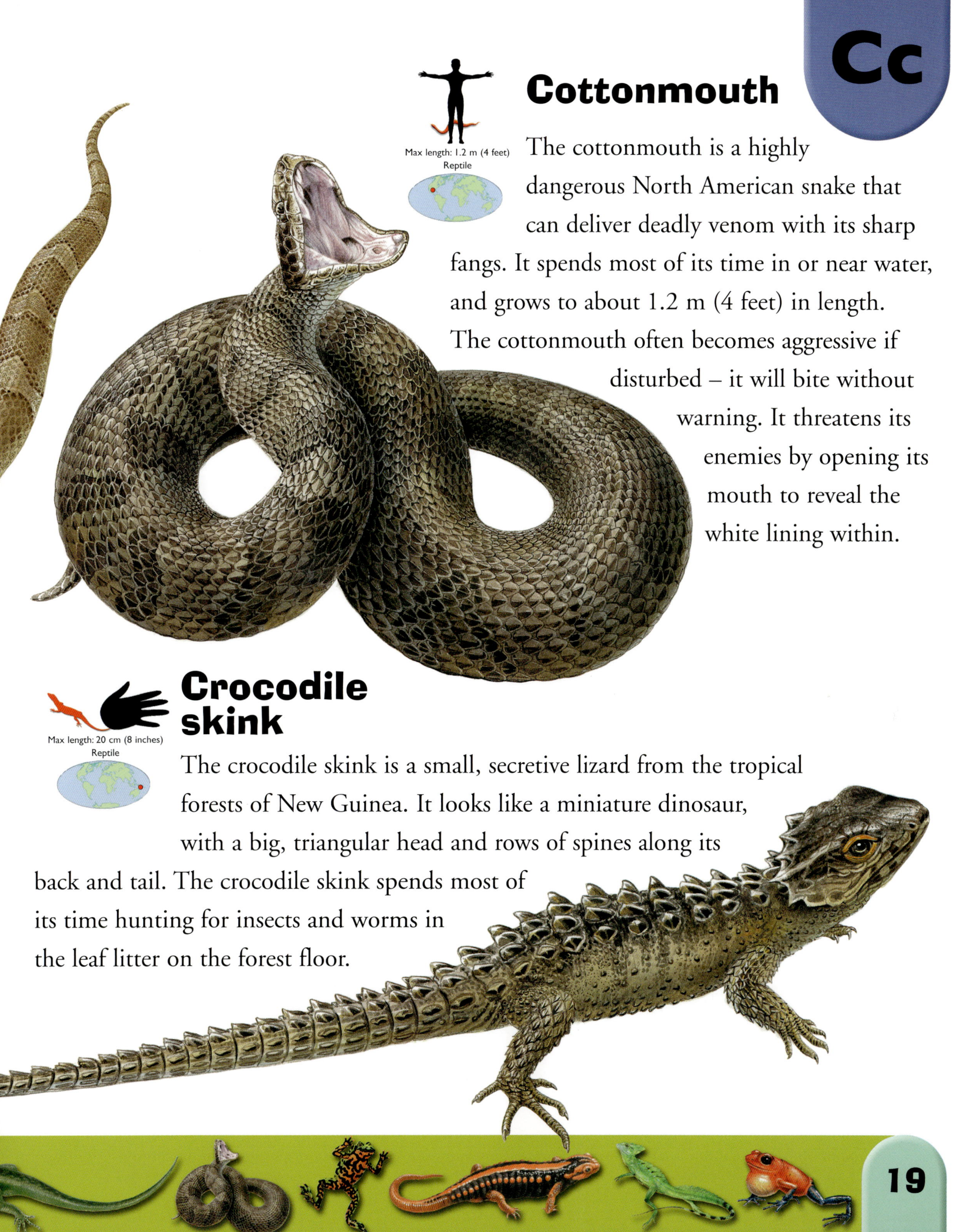

Cottonmouth

The cottonmouth is a highly dangerous North American snake that can deliver deadly venom with its sharp fangs. It spends most of its time in or near water, and grows to about 1.2 m (4 feet) in length. The cottonmouth often becomes aggressive if disturbed – it will bite without warning. It threatens its enemies by opening its mouth to reveal the white lining within.

Crocodile skink

The crocodile skink is a small, secretive lizard from the tropical forests of New Guinea. It looks like a miniature dinosaur, with a big, triangular head and rows of spines along its back and tail. The crocodile skink spends most of its time hunting for insects and worms in the leaf litter on the forest floor.

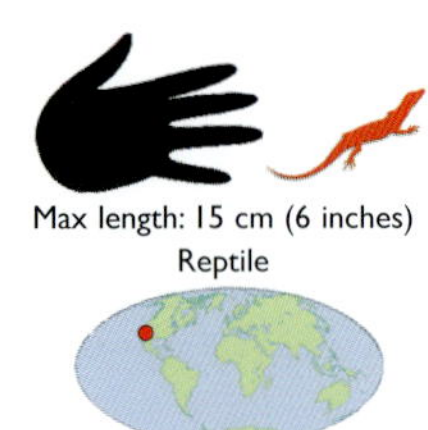

Desert horned lizard

The desert horned lizard is a small desert animal. It is commonly called a 'horned toad' even though it is a reptile, not an amphibian. It has a wide, flat body with a short tail, and it feeds mainly on ants that it gathers up with its tongue. When threatened, the desert horned lizard is able to squirt blood from its eye sockets.

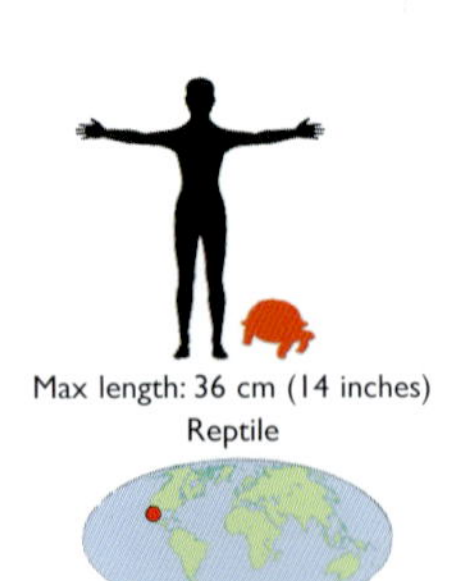

Desert tortoise

The desert tortoise is found in the southwestern United States and northern Mexico. This reptile shelters from hot and cold extremes by digging deep burrows that can be 10 m (33 feet) long. These burrows also provide shelter for other creatures. The desert tortoise feeds on cacti, herbs, grasses and certain shrubs.

Fact

During the mating season, desert tortoises can be very aggressive and males will attack each other on sight.

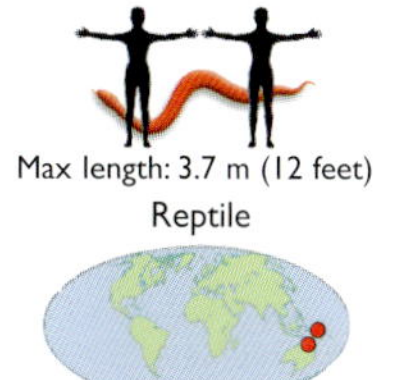

Diamond python

The diamond python lives in tropical forests and grassland in Australia and New Guinea. This non-venomous snake reaches a maximum length of about 3.7 m (12 feet) when full-grown. The diamond python feeds on small mammals and birds. It suffocates its victims inside its muscular coils before swallowing them whole.

Max length: 1.9 m (6¼ feet)
Reptile

Dwarf crocodile

The dwarf crocodile is found in swampy regions of tropical rainforest in central Africa. Although it is small compared to the Nile crocodile, it is still a large reptile. When the forest is flooded, it eats fish. When the water levels are lower, this crocodile feeds on crustaceans and frogs.

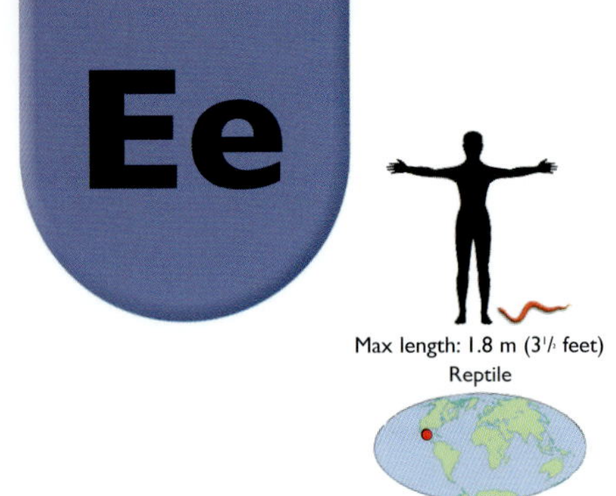

Max length: 1.8 m (3½ feet)
Reptile

Eastern glass lizard

The eastern glass lizard looks like a snake but it is, in fact, a legless lizard with a long tail. Found in the southeastern United States, it grows to about 1.8 m (3½ feet) long. It gets its name because when it is attacked by a predator, its long tail detaches from its body – breaking like glass.

Max length: 11.5 cm (4½ inches)
Amphibian

Eastern newt

The eastern newt is also known as the red-spotted newt. This small amphibian is widespread in eastern North America. Its tadpoles do not develop directly into adults, but go through a land-living juvenile stage. During this time, they are known as red efts. It can take up to four years for a red eft to develop into an adult eastern newt.

Max length: 25 cm (10 inches)
Reptile

Emerald tree skink

The emerald tree skink is found in New Guinea and on many other islands in the Pacific Ocean. This small reptile hunts for insects high in the branches of tropical forests. Like many other lizards, its tail can detach and carry on wiggling to distract an attacker, while the lizard makes its escape.

European fire salamander

Max length: 28 cm (11 inches)
Amphibian

The European fire salamander lives in damp, hillside forests. During the day it is most often found in the rotting interiors of fallen trees. At night it comes out to feed on insects, slugs and worms. Its bright colouration warns predators that this amphibian is poisonous to eat. Special glands on the salamander's head produce toxic chemicals, and it can spray them several metres.

Eyelash pit viper

Max length: 76 cm (2½ feet)
Reptile

The eyelash pit viper is a tree-dwelling snake from the tropical forests of Central America. It gets its name from a ridge of raised scales above each eye that look like eyelashes. It grows to about 76 cm (2½ feet) and feeds on small mammals, amphibians and lizards. The eyelash pit viper can strike fast enough to grab a hummingbird in mid-air.

Fire-bellied toad

Max length: 5 cm (2 inches)
Amphibian

The oriental fire-bellied toad, like the European fire salamander, gets its name from its bright colouration. When threatened, the toad throws itself on its back, revealing the bright colours of its underside. These colours warn predators that this toad is poisonous – it releases toxic substances through its skin.

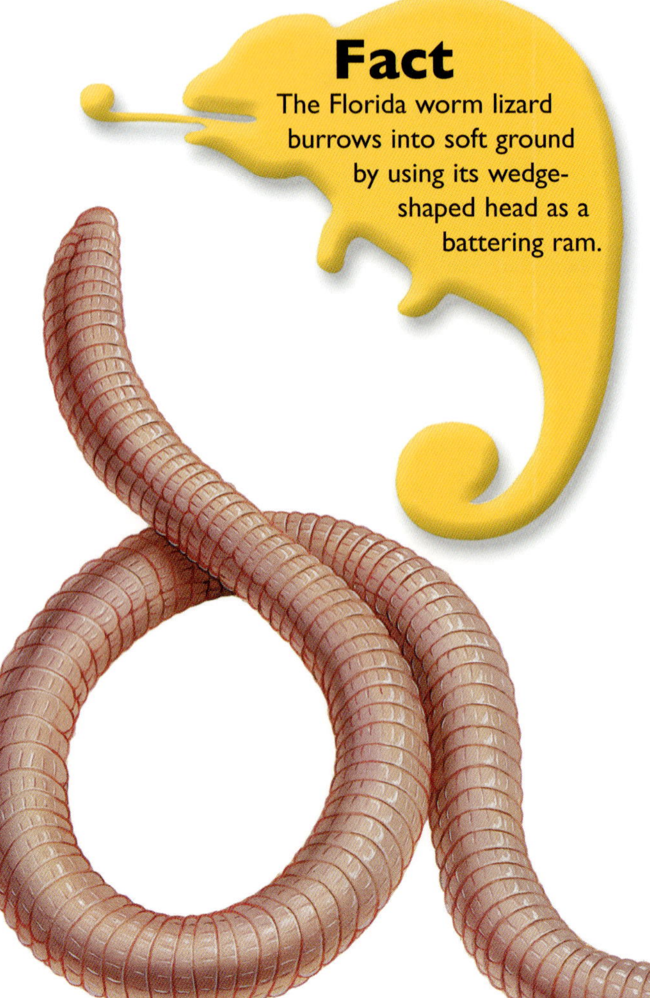

Max length: 36 cm (14 inches)
Reptile

Florida worm lizard

The Florida worm lizard is related to the ajolote of Mexico but, like most worm lizards, it has no legs at all. The scales of this unusual reptile are arranged in rings around its body, making it look like an earthworm. The Florida worm lizard grows to about 36 cm (14 inches) long and spends most of its life underground, feeding on invertebrates.

Flying lizard

Max length: 20 cm (8 inches)
Reptile

The flying lizard is a common sight on some islands in Southeast Asia. It can glide between forest trees on 'wings' that extend from the sides of its body. These wings are made from skin stretched over elongated ribs. They are folded against the body while the flying lizard is hunting for ants among the branches.

Frilled lizard

Max length: 70 cm (2¹/₄ feet)
Reptile

The frilled lizard of Australia and New Guinea has one of the most spectacular defences of any animal on Earth. This medium-sized reptile has a frill of skin that normally hangs around the animal's neck and shoulders. When threatened by a bird of prey, the lizard raises its frill, which makes its head look about five times bigger. The frilled lizard adds to the effect by opening its mouth wide and hissing.

Galapagos tortoise

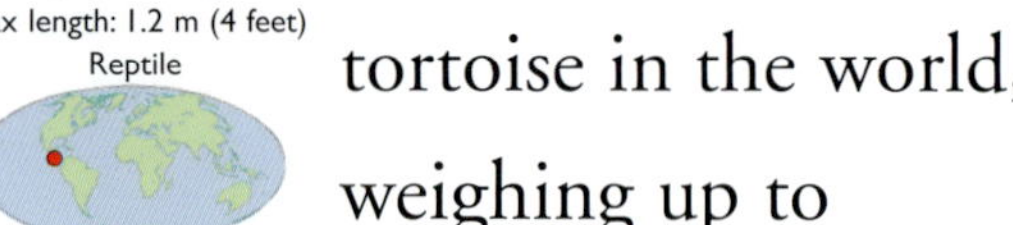

The Galapagos tortoise is the biggest tortoise in the world, weighing up to 350 kg (770 lbs). It is only found on the remote Galapagos Islands. This tortoise can go without food and water for up to a year because it is able to store energy for long periods.

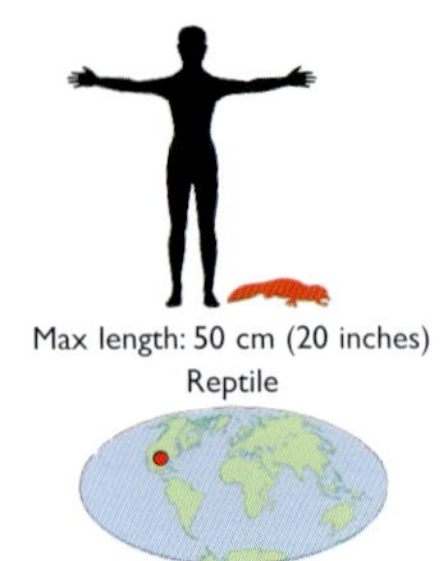

Gila monster

The gila monster is one of only two lizards in the world that has a venomous bite (the other is the Mexican beaded lizard). It is a desert reptile and it feeds mostly on small mammals and birds' eggs. It can go a long time between meals because it stores fat in its tail and abdomen. It moves slowly, but has a very powerful bite.

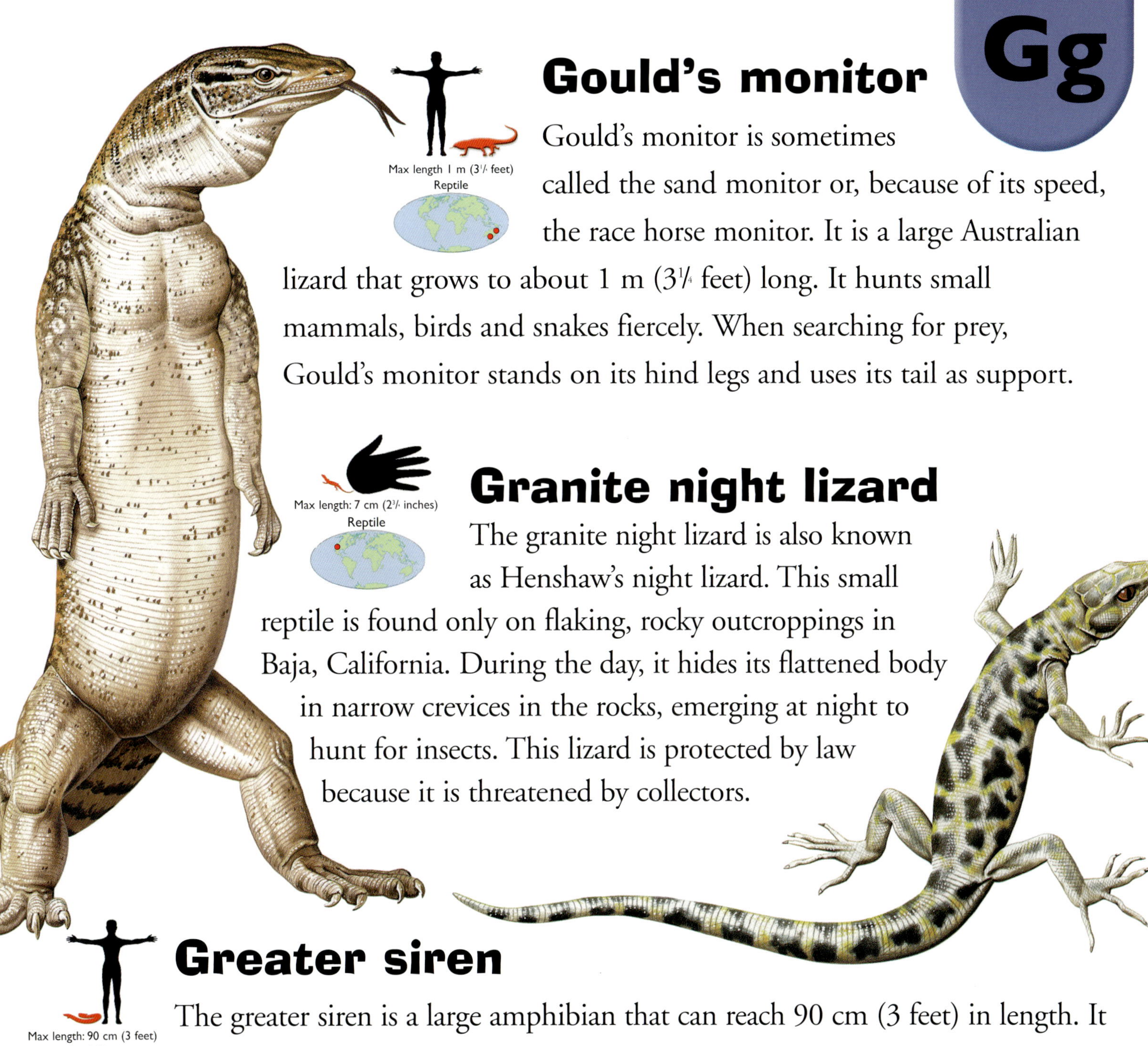

Gould's monitor

Gould's monitor is sometimes called the sand monitor or, because of its speed, the race horse monitor. It is a large Australian lizard that grows to about 1 m (3¼ feet) long. It hunts small mammals, birds and snakes fiercely. When searching for prey, Gould's monitor stands on its hind legs and uses its tail as support.

Granite night lizard

The granite night lizard is also known as Henshaw's night lizard. This small reptile is found only on flaking, rocky outcroppings in Baja, California. During the day, it hides its flattened body in narrow crevices in the rocks, emerging at night to hunt for insects. This lizard is protected by law because it is threatened by collectors.

Max length: 90 cm (3 feet)
Amphibian

Greater siren

The greater siren is a large amphibian that can reach 90 cm (3 feet) in length. It is found in shallow, muddy waters in the eastern United States. The greater siren uses gills on the outside of its head for breathing throughout its life. It has only one pair of legs at the front of its body. During dry periods it burrows into mud, where it can remain for up to two years.

Green anole

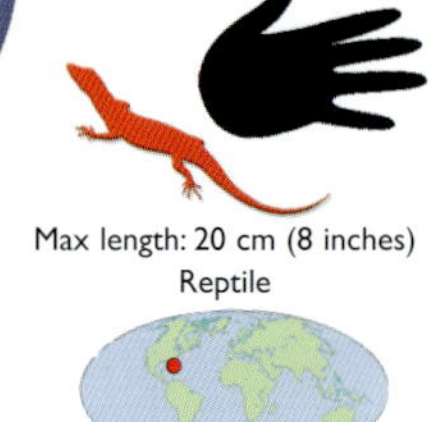

Max length: 20 cm (8 inches)
Reptile

The green anole is a small North American lizard that is sometimes mistakenly called a chameleon. It lives in warm forests where it hunts insects among the tree branches. A male green anole has a brightly coloured pouch under its throat. It can inflate this pouch as a signal to others of its kind.

Green-blooded skink

Max length: 15 cm (6 inches)
Reptile

The green-blooded skink is a small, tree-dwelling reptile from the remote mountain forests of New Guinea. There are five species of green-blooded skink. These five lizards are the only land animals – out of more than 24,000 mammals, birds, reptiles and amphibians – that have green blood. They are entirely green: they have green tongues, green bones and even green egg shells.

Fact

Scientists believe that the colour of the green-blooded skink comes from the chemicals that make it taste bitter when eaten.

Max length: 90 cm (3 feet)
Reptile

Hawksbill turtle

The hawksbill turtle is a small sea turtle that grows to no more than about 90 cm (3 feet) long. It lives in the warmer parts of the oceans, especially around coral reefs, where it feeds on sponges and shellfish. The hawksbill turtle has been hunted almost to extinction for its beautifully patterned carapace (shell).

Max length: 74 cm (2½ feet)
Amphibian

Hellbender

The hellbender is a large salamander with wrinkled skin. It is found in mountain streams in eastern North America, and it is sometimes called the Allegheny alligator. The hellbender feeds on invertebrates that it digs up from the stream bed. Despite its scary name, this amphibian is harmless.

Helmeted iguana

The helmeted iguana is a medium-sized reptile from the tropical forests of Central America. It gets its name from the narrow 'helmet' on the back of its head. The helmeted iguana can change its colour to match its surroundings. This iguana is sometimes called a basilisk.

Horned adder

The horned adder is a small, venomous snake found in the deserts of southern Africa. When full-grown, it measures about 50 cm (20 inches). The horned adder has rough scales that help it burrow into loose sand during the day to escape the desert sun. It emerges in the evening to hunt lizards and small mammals.

Ibiza wall lizard

Max length: 21 cm (8½ inches)
Reptile

The Ibiza wall lizard is a small reptile found on Mediterranean islands near the coast of Spain. Its long toes help it climb quickly over walls and rocks in search of insect prey. Ibiza wall lizards gather to sun themselves on sheltered slopes in groups of up to 50 individuals.

Indian cobra

Max length: 2.1 m (7 feet)
Reptile

The Indian cobra is also known as the spectacled cobra. This large, venomous snake has markings that look like eyes on the back of its 'hood'. It feeds mainly on small mammals and birds. This species is extremely dangerous and kills hundreds of people each year. Indian cobras live in the grass and farmlands of India and Pakistan.

Indian starred tortoise

Max length: 28 cm (11 inches)
Reptile

The Indian starred tortoise is a medium-sized reptile that lives in scrub jungles and other dry areas. Its name comes from the star pattern on its shell. Each of the inner plates rises to a tall, rounded point. These points make the carapace much stronger – and far more difficult for a predator to crush.

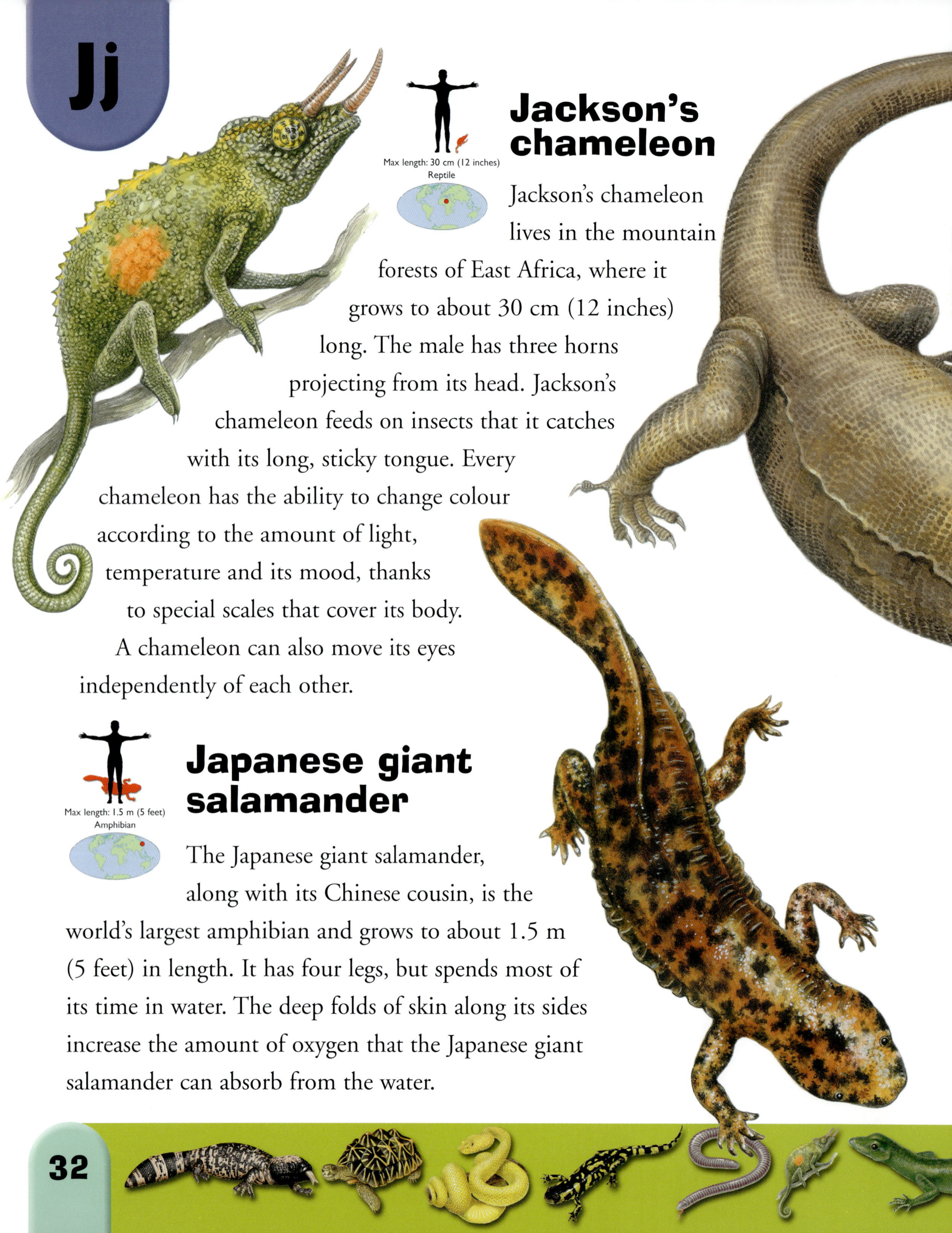

Jackson's chameleon

Jackson's chameleon lives in the mountain forests of East Africa, where it grows to about 30 cm (12 inches) long. The male has three horns projecting from its head. Jackson's chameleon feeds on insects that it catches with its long, sticky tongue. Every chameleon has the ability to change colour according to the amount of light, temperature and its mood, thanks to special scales that cover its body. A chameleon can also move its eyes independently of each other.

Japanese giant salamander

The Japanese giant salamander, along with its Chinese cousin, is the world's largest amphibian and grows to about 1.5 m (5 feet) in length. It has four legs, but spends most of its time in water. The deep folds of skin along its sides increase the amount of oxygen that the Japanese giant salamander can absorb from the water.

Kingsnake

Max length: 2.1 m (7 feet)
Reptile

The common kingsnake is a medium-sized snake that can reach 2.1 m (7 feet) in length. There are a number of subspecies, each with its own pattern and colouration. The common kingsnake is an aggressive predator that kills its prey by constriction. It feeds on small mammals, birds and other reptiles – it will even attack venomous snakes because other snakes' venom has no effect on the kingsnake.

Komodo dragon

Max length: 3 m (10 feet)
Reptile

The Komodo dragon is the world's biggest lizard. A male can weigh more than 100 kg (220 lbs). With powerful jaws and sharp claws, the Komodo dragon is a fierce hunter and has been known to bring down deer and even water buffalo. It can run at speeds of up to 18 km/h (11 mph) for short periods of time.

Kuhl's flying gecko

Max length: 20 cm (8 inches)
Reptile

Kuhl's flying gecko is a small lizard from the forests of Southeast Asia. It is well camouflaged for life in the trees and spends most of its time hunting for insects. When threatened, it can glide from branch to branch, thanks to its webbed feet and flaps of skin along its body and back legs. Kuhl's flying gecko uses its wavy-edged tail to control the direction of its glide.

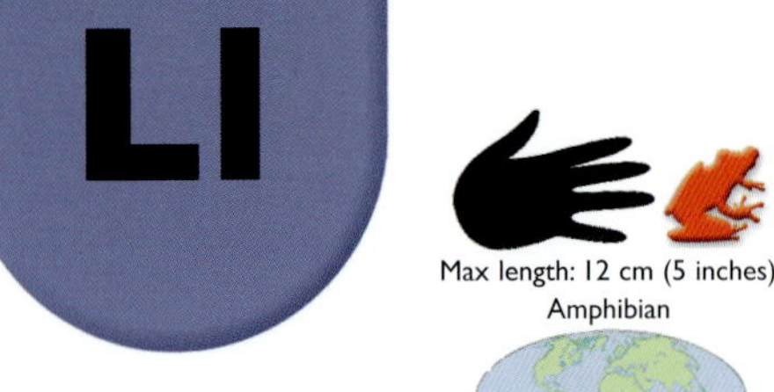

Lake Titicaca frog

The Lake Titicaca frog is the world's highest-living amphibian. It is found only around Lake Titicaca, which is some 3,800 m (12,500 feet) above sea level. At this height, both air and water are low in oxygen. As well as having a pair of lungs, the Lake Titicaca frog absorbs oxygen over the entire surface of its skin.

Max length: 12 cm (5 inches)
Amphibian

Leopard frog

The North American leopard frog is either green or brown in colour, with rows of irregular, dark spots. This small amphibian has a length of 12 cm (5 inches). It is often seen during the summer near ponds and streams. In the winter, the leopard frog remains hidden beneath rocks or fallen trees.

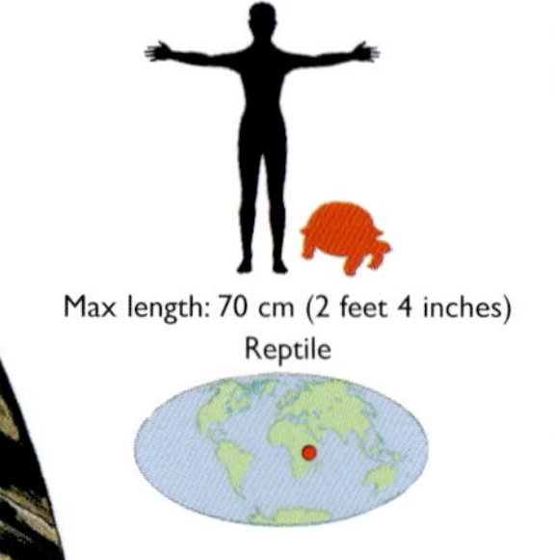

Leopard tortoise

The leopard tortoise is a medium-sized reptile that can reach just over 60 cm (2 feet) in length. It has a domed yellow carapace (shell) with dark markings. In some individuals, these markings look like a leopard's spots. The leopard tortoise feeds on low-growing plants and fallen fruit.

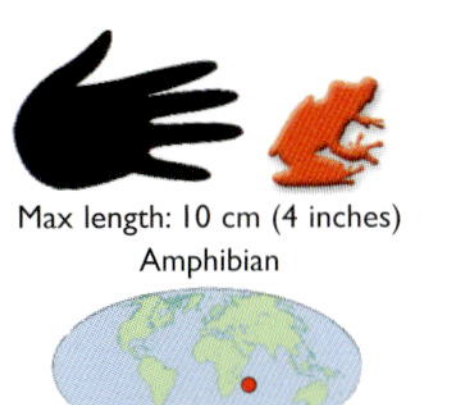

Madagascan tomato frog

The Madagascan tomato frog is a small, brightly coloured amphibian whose females can measure 10 cm (4 inches) long. It is found only in the remote northwestern corner of Madagascar, and was once seriously endangered by forest clearance. Tomato frogs hunt for food by sitting in one spot and waiting for an insect to pass by.

Fact

The black mamba is not actually black – it is either brown or grey. Its relative the green mamba really is green.

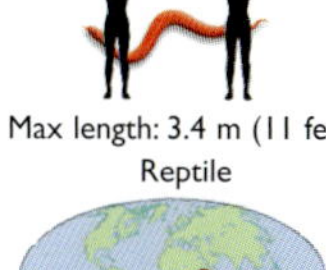

Mamba (black)

The black mamba is the world's fastest-moving snake. It can race across the ground at speeds of up to 19 km/h (12 mph). It is an excellent tree-climber and may strike at its victims from the branches. It is an extremely dangerous snake because of its deadly venom and speed. The black mamba gets its name because the inside of its mouth is black.

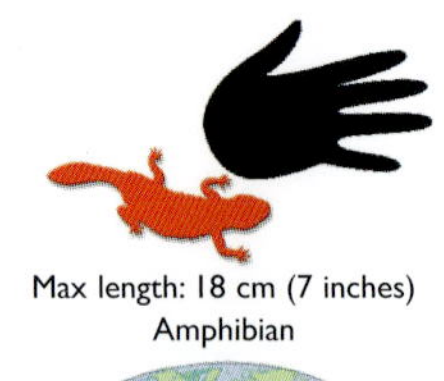

Mandarin salamander

The mandarin salamander is also known as the crocodile salamander. Its distinctive black and orange markings make it look like a crocodile. This small amphibian is found mainly in damp woodland, where it burrows into the ground in search of earthworms and other soft-bodied prey.

Fact

The mandarin salamander approaches prey very slowly. Then, it grabs its victim with a quick sideways movement of its head.

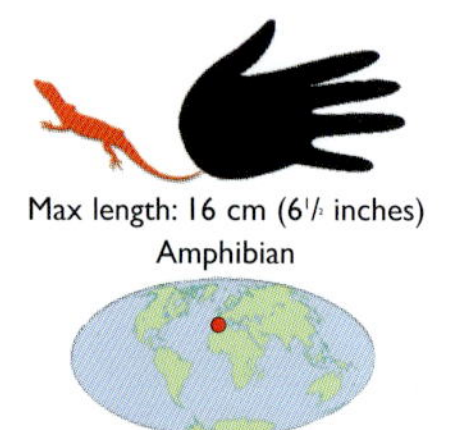

Marbled newt

The marbled newt is found in lakes, ponds and slow-moving rivers in southwestern Europe. This amphibian can reach 16 cm (6½ inches) in length, and has a distinctive crest along its back and tail. It has a black and green marbled colouring.

Max length: 1 m (3¼ feet)
Reptile

Marine iguana

The marine iguana is one of the strangest of all reptiles. This medium-sized lizard lives on the Galapagos Islands, where it dives into the sea to feed underwater on algae. The marine iguana often has a 'whitewashed' face. When it feeds, salt is taken into its body. Salt crystals are 'sneezed' from glands near its nostrils, producing this white colour.

Max length: 45 cm (18 inches)
Reptile

Matamata

The matamata is a freshwater turtle from the muddy rivers and ponds in the tropical forests of South America. This reptile has a flat, triangular head. The matamata hides beneath the surface of shallow water, breathing through nostrils at the tip of its long snout. Frills of skin on its neck help it detect the approach of prey, such as fish and amphibians.

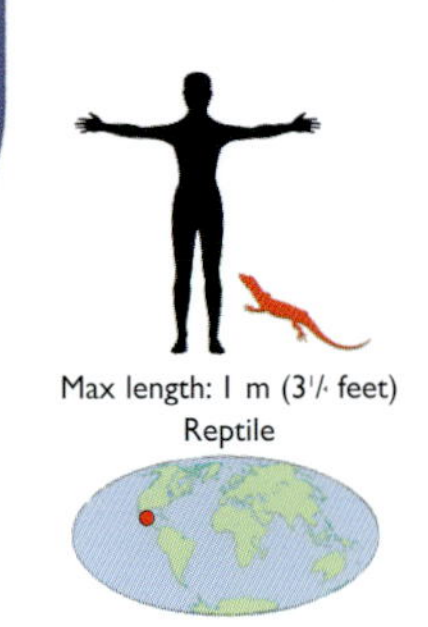

Mexican beaded lizard

The Mexican beaded lizard is one of only two venomous lizards – the other is the gila monster. Both species are found in the deserts of southwestern North America. The Mexican beaded lizard has the same rounded scales as the gila monster, but has a duller colour. It has powerful front legs for burrowing beneath the desert surface.

Max length: 49 cm (19½ inches)
Amphibian

Mudpuppy

The mudpuppy is widespread across North America and grows up to 49 cm (19½ inches) long. Like the greater siren, it lives in water for most of its life and breathes through large, feathery gills on the sides of its head. The mudpuppy is very sensitive to water quality, resulting in its disappearance from many polluted rivers.

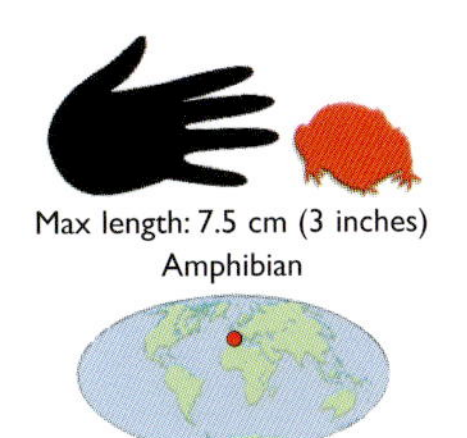

Natterjack toad

The natterjack toad is a small European amphibian that grows to about 7.5 cm (3 inches) long. It has a dark colouring with a yellow stripe along the centre of its back. The natterjack toad prefers open landscapes with sandy soil, and is sometimes found near coastal sand dunes. The natterjack tends to run instead of hopping like other toads.

Nile crocodile

Max length: 6 m (20 feet)
Reptile

The Nile crocodile is a very dangerous reptile that can grow to 6 m (20 feet) in length. It feeds by ambushing prey at the edges of rivers and lakes. The Nile crocodile attacks and eats prey as large as zebra or water buffalo. It drags its victim underwater to drown it.

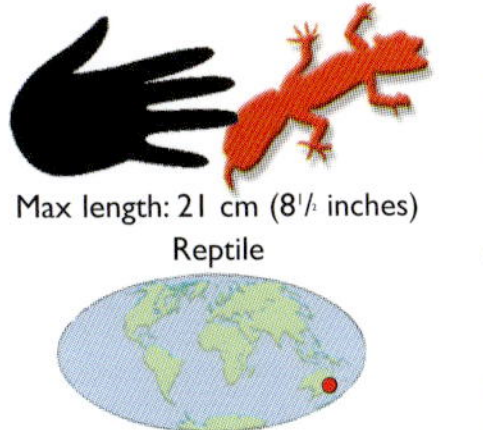

Northern leaf-tailed gecko

The northern leaf-tailed gecko is a small reptile that lives in the tropical forests of northern and eastern Australia. This gecko's body is flat, making no shadow, and is camouflaged to look like the bark of a tree. This 'woody' appearance continues along its leaf-shaped tail, which can be dropped and regrown.

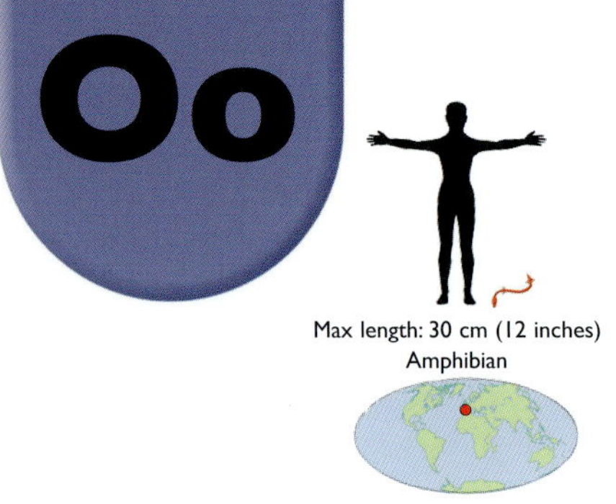

Olm

The olm is a strange salamander, found only in certain caves in southern Europe. This amphibian has become adapted to life in complete darkness. Its skin has almost no colour, and it has nearly lost the use of its eyes. The olm uses its sense of smell to hunt for small invertebrates in underground streams.

Max length: 20 cm (8 inches)
Amphibian

Ornate horned toad

The ornate horned toad is a fat-bodied amphibian that grows to about 20 cm (8 inches) in length. It spends most of its time on the ground, half-buried among fallen leaves and moss, waiting for prey to approach. When a mouse or small lizard comes too close, the toad opens its wide mouth – full of large, sharp teeth – and swallows its prey in one gulp.

Fact
The ornate patterns that give this toad its name are a highly effective form of camouflage.

Pacific giant salamander

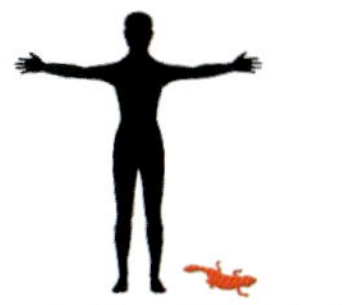

Max length: 34 cm (13½ inches)
Amphibian

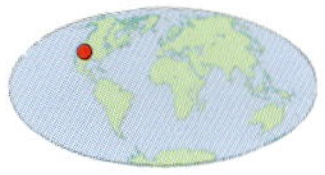

The Pacific giant salamander is an amphibian from the damp forests along the western coast of North America. When full-grown, it can reach 34cm (13½ inches) in length. Some individuals spend their entire lives in water, breathing through feathery gills. Others leave the water after a few years and develop lungs. Those that leave the water are among the largest salamanders that live on land.

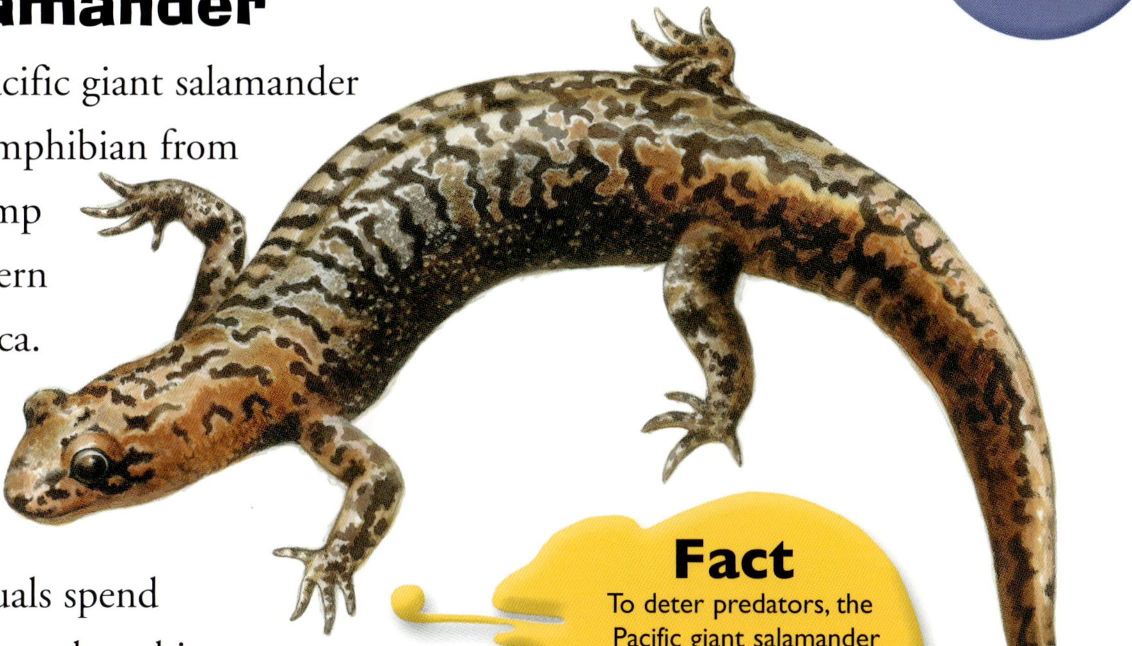

Fact

To deter predators, the Pacific giant salamander exudes a foul-smelling liquid from its tail .

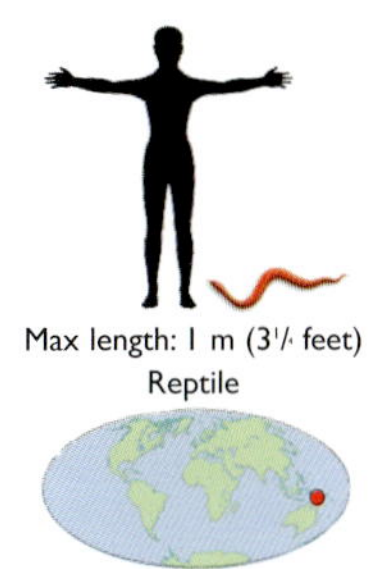

Pacific ground boa

Max length: 1 m (3½ feet)
Reptile

The Pacific ground boa from New Guinea has two subspecies. One is fat-bodied and hunts prey on the ground. The other subspecies has a narrower body and spends most of its time in the trees. The Pacific ground boa is non-venomous and kills its prey by constriction.

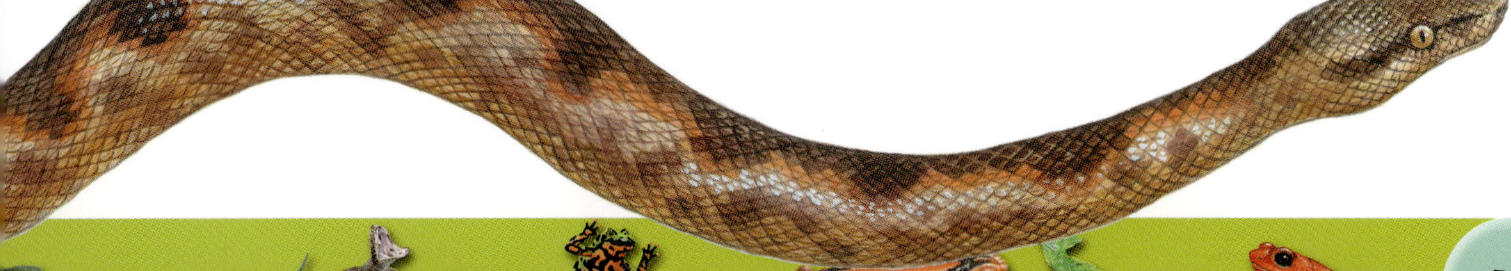

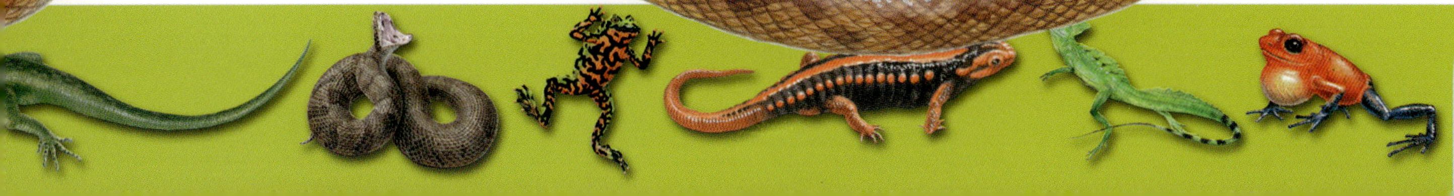

Max length: 25 cm (10 inches)
Reptile

Painted turtle

The painted turtle is widespread in North America, where it grows to about 25 cm (10 inches) long. It is often seen on rocks and logs in the mornings, warming itself in the sunlight. When threatened by a predator, such as a raccoon, the painted turtle pulls its head back into its carapace.

Fact
Young painted turtles are meat eaters, but as they grow up, they become vegetarian, or plant eaters.

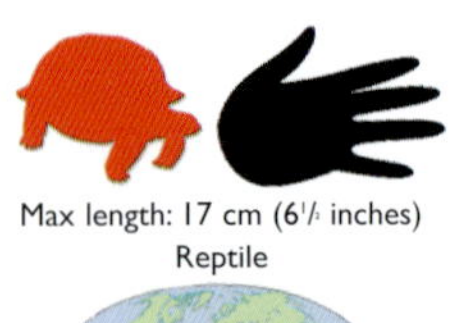

Max length: 17 cm (6½ inches)
Reptile

Pancake tortoise

The pancake tortoise is a small African reptile about 17 cm (6½ inches) long. It has a very flat carapace (shell) with plates that are flexible, not fixed in a rigid shape. This flexible shell allows the pancake tortoise to squeeze itself beneath rocks to hide from birds of prey and other predators.

Pine snake

The pine snake, found only in the southeastern United States, grows up to 2.5 m (8¼ feet). It is also known as the gopher snake because it burrows underground to hunt for small mammals, such as gophers. The pine snake is non-venomous, but will hiss and strike like a venomous snake.

Plumed basilisk

The plumed basilisk is a medium-sized lizard from Central America. It is easily identifiable by the crests along its back and tail and its huge head crest. The plumed basilisk lives in trees near rivers and ponds. When threatened by a predator, it escapes by running on its back legs for short distances across the water's surface.

Qq Rr

Queensland cane toad

Max length: 3 cm (29 inches)
Amphibian

The Queensland cane toad is also known as the marine toad. This aggressive amphibian lives in the tropical forests of South and Central America. It was introduced to Queensland, Australia, to combat insect pests that were attacking the sugar cane crop. A cane toad will eat almost anything it can swallow.

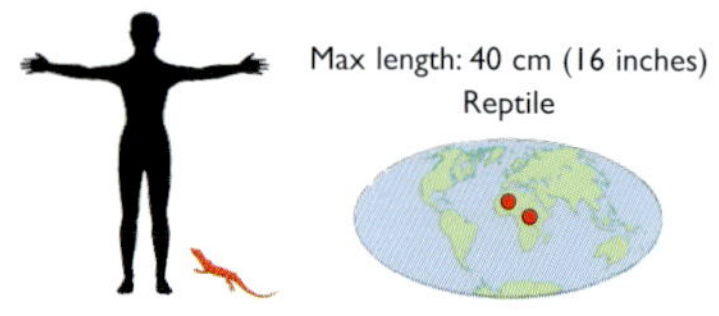

Rainbow lizard

The rainbow lizard is a medium-sized reptile that is widespread across central Africa. When full-grown, it measures about 40 cm (16 inches) long. Only males have the bright red and blue colouration that give this lizard its name – females and juveniles are dull grey. At night, the males turn grey, but when their bodies warm up in the morning sunlight, they become coloured again.

Fact

Male rainbow lizards fight each other using sideways blows of the tail. The defeated male turns a dull grey colour.

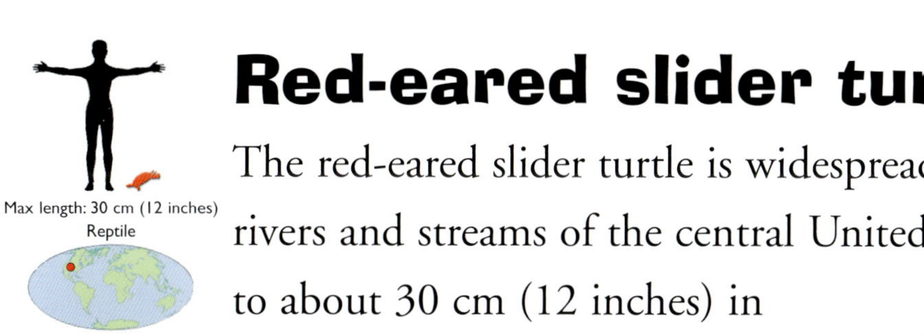

Red-eared slider turtle

The red-eared slider turtle is widespread in the lakes, rivers and streams of the central United States. It grows to about 30 cm (12 inches) in length. Its red 'ears' are, in fact, a pair of distinctive red stripes, one behind each eye. The red-eared turtle likes to bask in warm sunlight. Sometimes these turtles climb on top of each other – in a stack – in their efforts to get to the very best basking position.

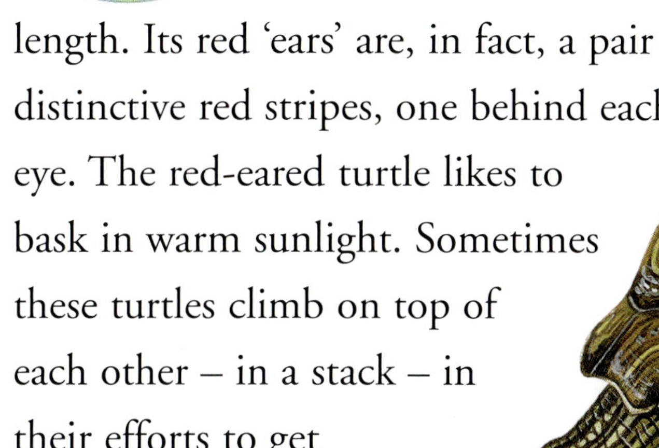

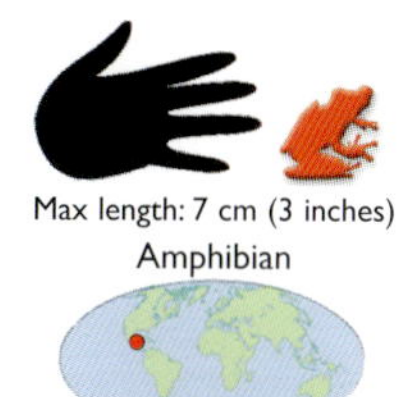

Red-eyed tree frog

The red-eyed tree frog is a small amphibian from South and Central America that spends most of its life in the trees. In the breeding season, it lays eggs on leaves above small ponds. When the tadpoles hatch, they drop into the water. It has brightly coloured markings on its sides, which can be covered by its green legs for good camouflage.

Rr

Red spitting cobra

The red spitting cobra is a venomous snake from eastern Africa that measures up to 1.2 m (4 feet). It has a very special method of attacking its prey. It does not bite its victims to inject its venom. Instead, it sprays a cloud of venomous droplets up to 1.8 m (6 feet) into the eyes of its prey. The venom causes instant blindness and makes the prey helpless.

Reinwardt's flying frog

Reinwardt's flying frog is found in the tropical forests of Indonesia. Like some of its close relatives, it has developed the ability to 'fly' or 'glide' between tree branches. Reinwardt's flying frog has large back feet with wide webs of skin between the toes. These webs act like parachutes as the frog glides through the air.

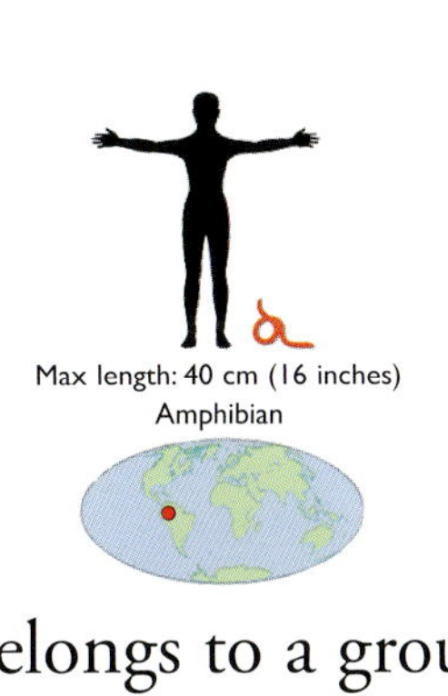

Ringed caecilian

The ringed caecilian is also known as the South American caecilian. It belongs to a group of amphibians – the caecilians – that are rarely seen because they live underground or, sometimes, under the mud at the bottom of lakes. The ringed caecilian has distinctive pale rings around its wormlike body. Caecilians may look like worms, but they have sharp, needle-like teeth.

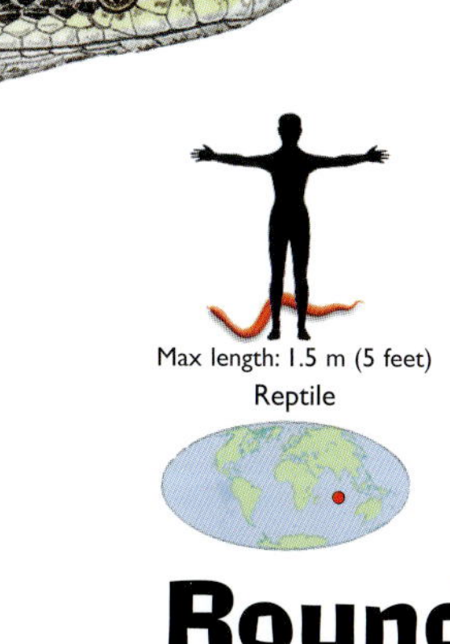

Round Island keel-scaled boa

The Round Island keel-scaled boa is one of the world's rarest snakes, found only on a single small island in the Indian Ocean. It gets part of its name from the shape of its scales, each of which has a central ridge, known as a keel. Unlike most boas, which give birth to live young, the Round Island keel-scaled boa lays eggs.

Ss

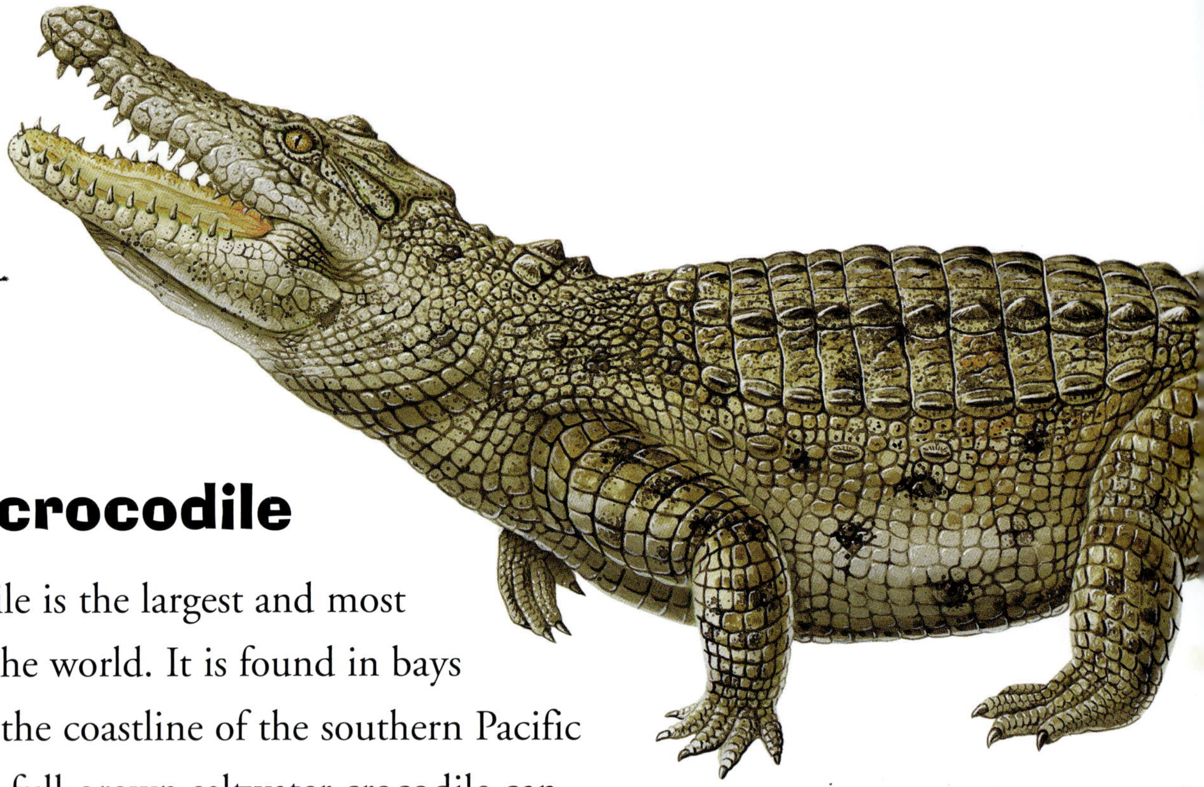

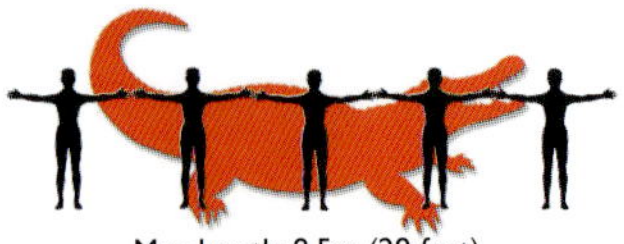

Max length: 8.5m (28 feet)
Reptile

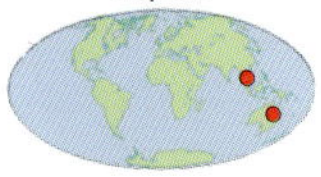

Saltwater crocodile

The saltwater crocodile is the largest and most dangerous reptile in the world. It is found in bays and estuaries around the coastline of the southern Pacific and Indian oceans. A full-grown saltwater crocodile can measure more than 8.5 m (28 feet) in length, and will eat almost anything it can overpower, including humans.

Max length: 1.8 m (6 feet)
Reptile

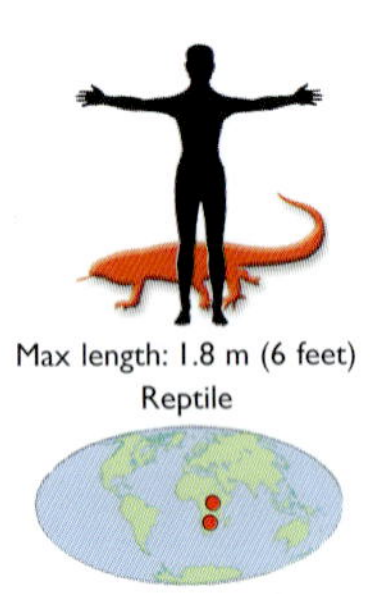

Savannah monitor

The Savannah monitor is a large lizard from the grasslands of Africa that can reach about 1.8 m (6 feet) in length. It is also known as the white-throated monitor.

When threatened, the savannah monitor puffs up its pale-coloured throat and body to make it look even bigger and more fierce. Then it whips its tail from side to side.

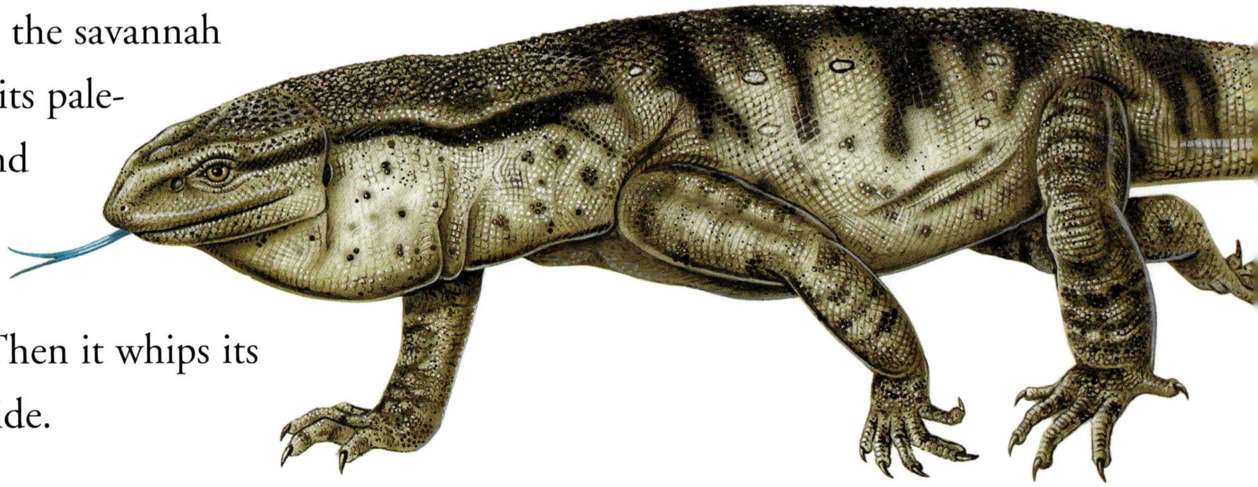

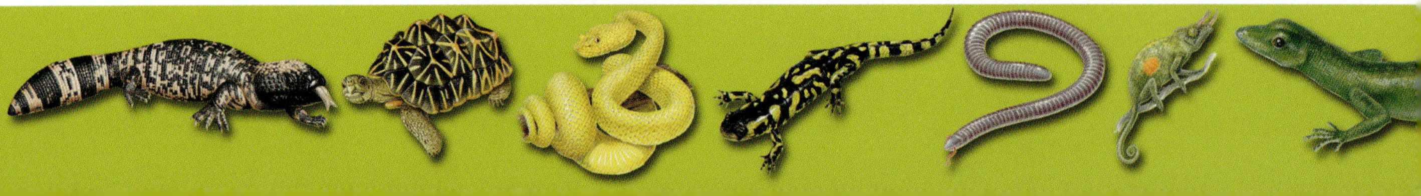

Max length: 32 cm (12½ inches)
Reptile

Serrated hinge-back tortoise

The serrated hinge-back tortoise is found in central Africa and prefers a forest habitat. This medium-sized reptile grows to just over 32 cm (12½ inches) in length. It gets its name from the design of its carapace (shell), which can be folded down to completely protect the animal inside. The sharp serrations around the edge of the carapace also help to deter predators.

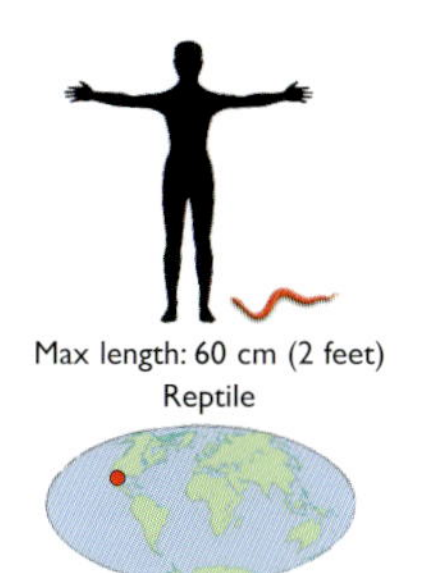

Sidewinder

The sidewinder is a large, venomous snake from the deserts of southwestern North America. Instead of slithering forwards head first like most snakes, the sidewinder moves across the ground in a series of sideways S-shapes. This method of movement means that only a small area of the snake's body is in contact with the hot surface of the desert.

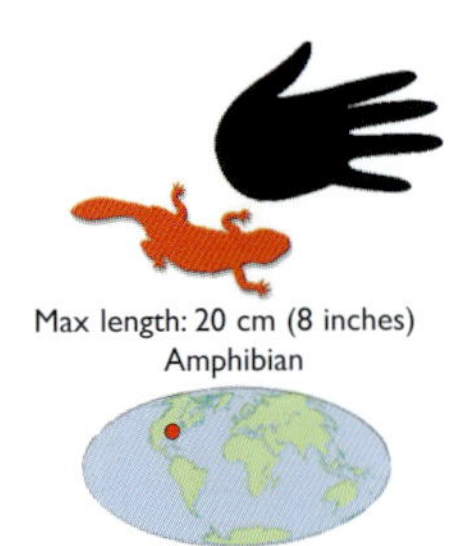

Slimy salamander

The slimy salamander is widespread in the eastern United States. This amphibian grows to about 20 cm (8 inches) in length. It has a dark-coloured body with white or silver spots, and it is only seen at night. As a defence, its skin produces a very sticky slime, which makes this animal an unpleasant mouthful for a predator.

Fact
One difference between slow worms and snakes is that a slow worm has movable eyelids and a snake does not.

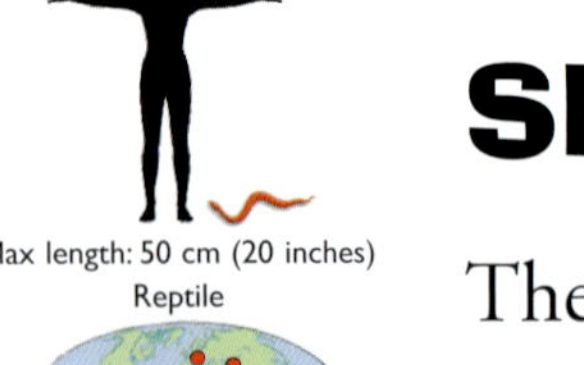

Slow worm

The slow worm is a legless lizard that is often mistaken for a snake. It measures about 50 cm (20 inches) long, and it is widespread across Europe. The slow worm spends most of its time under logs, stones and deep undergrowth, hunting for slugs and insects. Like some other lizards, it can shed its tail to escape from predators.

Snake-necked turtle

Max length: 25 cm (10 inches)
Reptile

The snake-necked turtle is found in the rivers of eastern Australia. The head and neck of this unusual reptile are often longer than the rest of its body. The snake-necked turtle shoots out its long neck to snatch passing fish. The long neck also allows the turtle to breathe at the surface while its body remains completely under water.

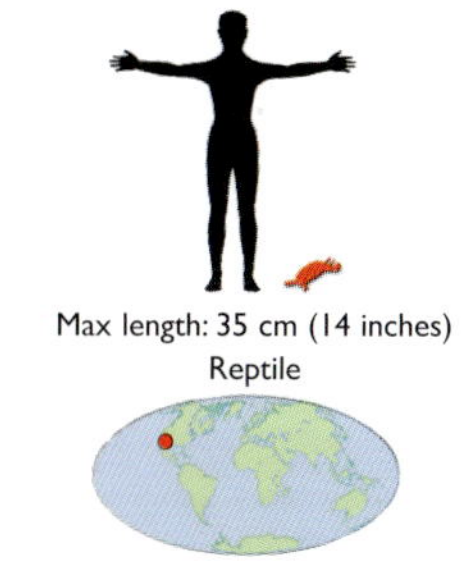
Max length: 35 cm (14 inches)
Reptile

Softshell turtle

The smooth softshell turtle is found in central parts of the United States. Unlike other turtles, it does not have a bony carapace (shell). Instead, its shell is covered with leathery skin. The softshell turtle often makes its nest on sandbars in the middle of slow-moving rivers. Females reach about 35 cm (14 inches) in length, but males are only half this size.

Ss

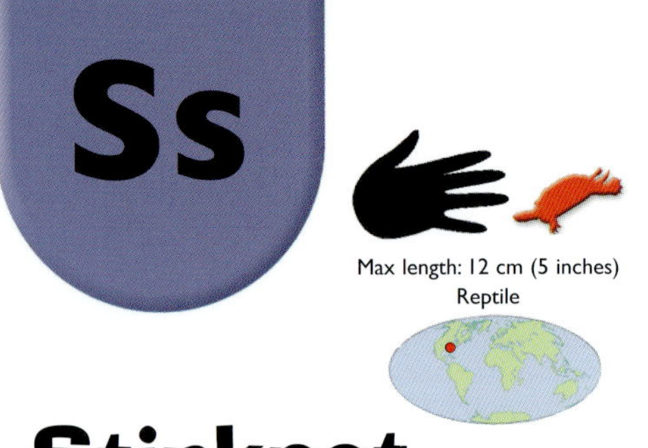

Stinkpot

The stinkpot is a small turtle from the southeastern United States about 12 cm (5 inches) long. Although it is small in size, it packs a very powerful and unpleasant surprise. When disturbed, the stinkpot releases a foul-smelling substance from special glands. It can also deliver a very painful bite.

Strawberry poison dart frog

The strawberry poison dart frog is one of the most brightly coloured amphibians. These tiny frogs are often spotted or striped, and they vary in colour depending on their location. These bright colours are a warning to predators that the frogs' skin is poisonous.

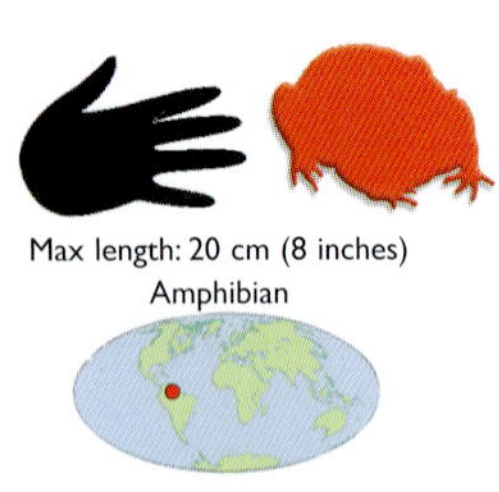

Surinam toad

The Surinam toad is found in South America, where it spends its entire life in water. It has a flattened body with a triangular head, and grows to about 20 cm (8 inches) in length. To help it find food in muddy water, the Surinam toad has special sense organs along its sides. It also has thin tentacles on the tips of its fingers to improve its sense of touch.

Texas blind snake

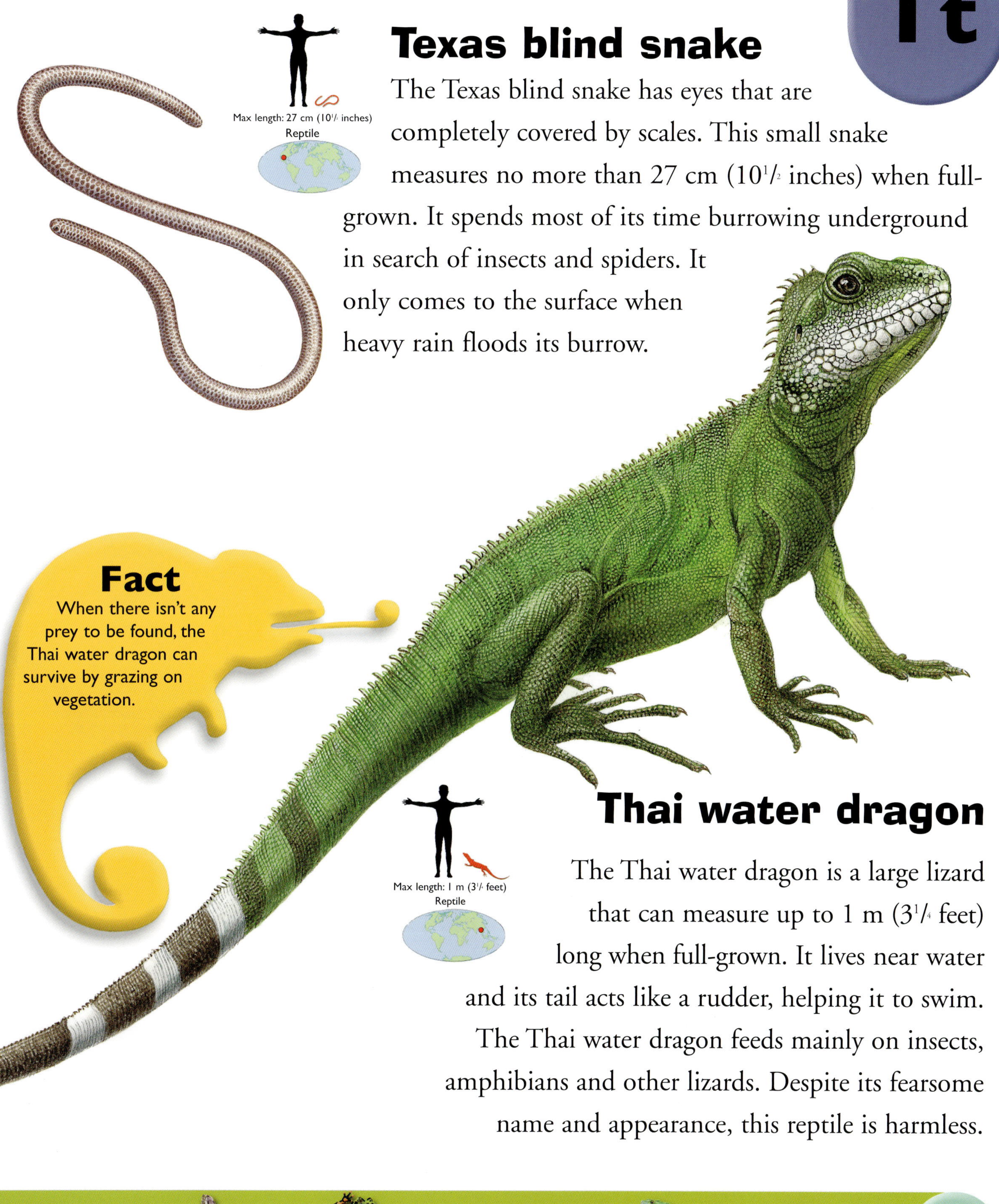

The Texas blind snake has eyes that are completely covered by scales. This small snake measures no more than 27 cm (10 1/2 inches) when full-grown. It spends most of its time burrowing underground in search of insects and spiders. It only comes to the surface when heavy rain floods its burrow.

Fact

When there isn't any prey to be found, the Thai water dragon can survive by grazing on vegetation.

Thai water dragon

The Thai water dragon is a large lizard that can measure up to 1 m (3 1/4 feet) long when full-grown. It lives near water and its tail acts like a rudder, helping it to swim. The Thai water dragon feeds mainly on insects, amphibians and other lizards. Despite its fearsome name and appearance, this reptile is harmless.

Tt

Thorny devil

The thorny devil is a lizard from the deserts of western Australia. This bizarre-looking reptile, only 18 cm (7 inches) long, is well camouflaged. The thorny devil moves very slowly and is unable to run away from predators. For protection, it relies on sharp spines that cover its head, body and tail.

Tiger salamander

The tiger salamander is widespread in North America. There are several subspecies, some of which have yellow and black markings, while others are mostly green or brown. When full-grown, the tiger salamander measures about 35 cm (14 inches) long. It rivals the Pacific giant salamander as the largest land-living salamander.

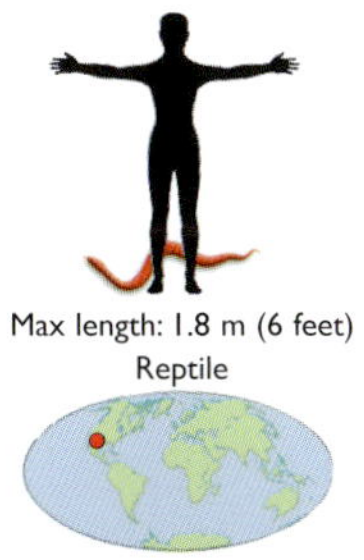

Max length: 1.8 m (6 feet)
Reptile

Trans-Pecos ratsnake

The Trans-Pecos ratsnake is found in the deserts of southwestern North America. This burrowing snake grows to about 1.8 m (6 feet) in length. During the day, the Trans-Pecos ratsnake shelters underground or beneath rocks. It comes out at night to hunt, when it uses its large eyes to find prey in the dark.

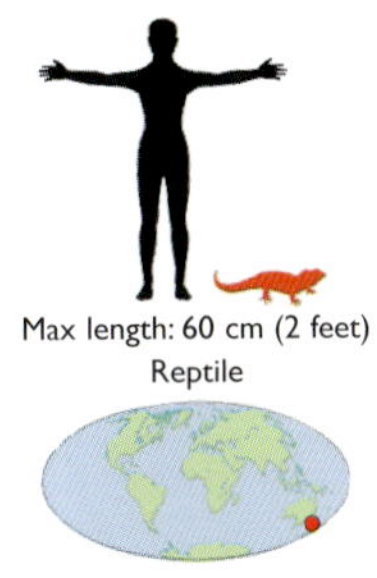

Max length: 60 cm (2 feet)
Reptile

Tuatara

The tuatara is an ancient and rare creature found on islands near the coast of New Zealand. It can reach about 60 cm (2 feet) in length and feeds on insects and worms. Although it looks like an iguana, it is part of a separate group of reptiles. Its scales and bone structures are more closely related to reptiles that became extinct over 200 million years ago.

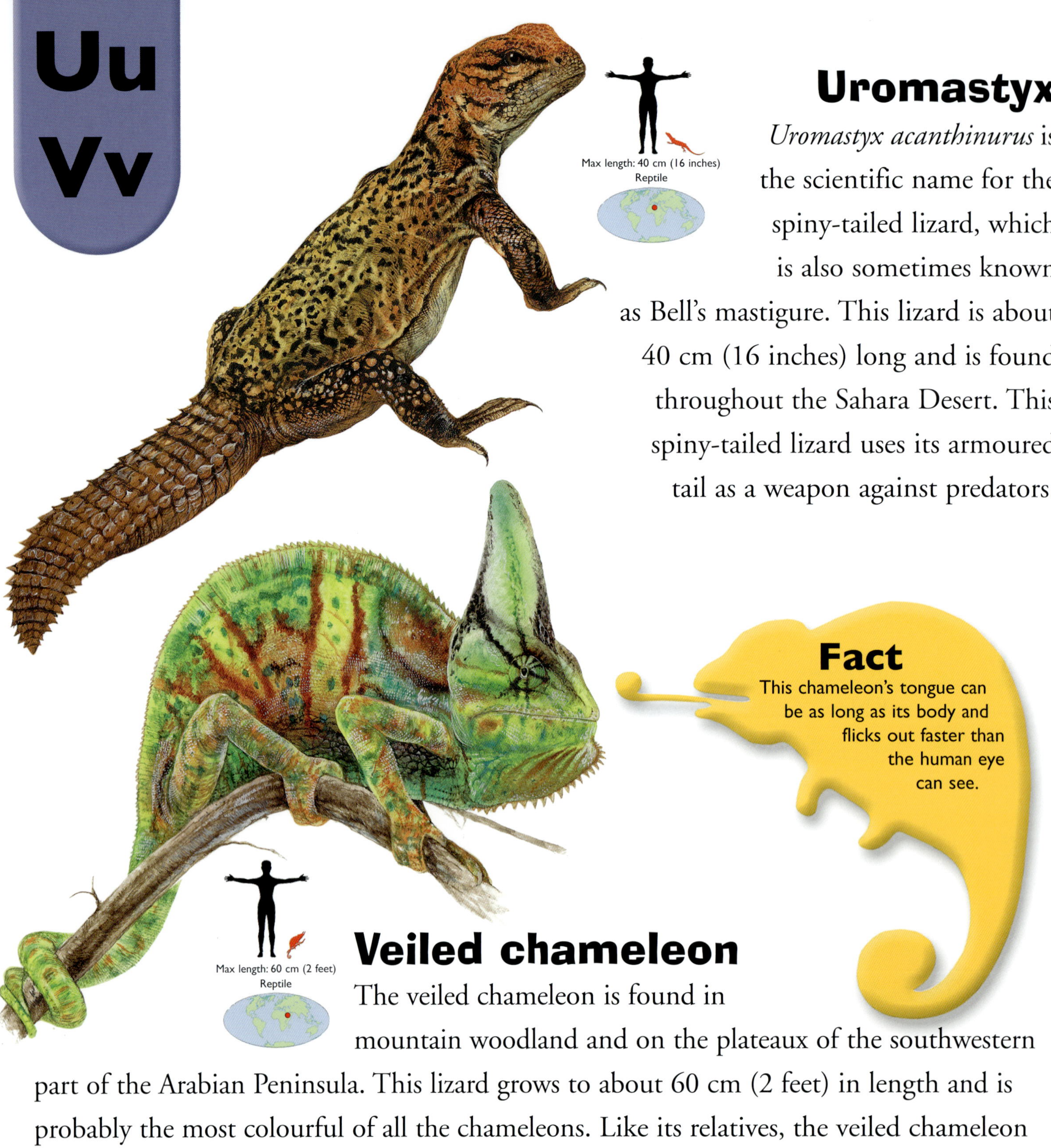

Uromastyx

Uromastyx acanthinurus is the scientific name for the spiny-tailed lizard, which is also sometimes known as Bell's mastigure. This lizard is about 40 cm (16 inches) long and is found throughout the Sahara Desert. This spiny-tailed lizard uses its armoured tail as a weapon against predators.

Fact

This chameleon's tongue can be as long as its body and flicks out faster than the human eye can see.

Veiled chameleon

The veiled chameleon is found in mountain woodland and on the plateaux of the southwestern part of the Arabian Peninsula. This lizard grows to about 60 cm (2 feet) in length and is probably the most colourful of all the chameleons. Like its relatives, the veiled chameleon can move each of its eyes independently, enabling it to look for prey in two directions at the same time. It feeds on insects and vegetation.

Web-footed gecko

The web-footed gecko is a small lizard that reaches about 14 cm (5½ inches) in length. It lives in the Namib Desert, where its webbed feet keep it from sinking into the sand. The web-footed gecko escapes the heat of the day in an underground burrow. It comes out at night to search for food and water.

Western diamondback rattlesnake

The western diamondback rattlesnake is one of the most dangerous snakes in North America. It has curved, hollow fangs that inject a deadly venom. The western diamondback rattlesnake can reach 2.1 m (7 feet) when full-grown. After a snake sheds its skin, the rattle gains a new section.

Wood turtle

The wood turtle lives along forested rivers and streams in North America. This small reptile grows to about 19 cm (7½ inches) in length. Although the wood turtle spends a lot of its time in the water, it often wanders through the woods in search of food, such as worms, insects, leaves and berries.

Xenopus laevis

Xenopus laevis is the scientific name for the African clawed frog. This amphibian is about 13 cm (5½ inches) long, and it spends most of its time at the bottom of muddy ponds and lakes. The African clawed frog has a row of special sense organs along its sides. These organs help it to detect prey, and this frog will eat almost anything.

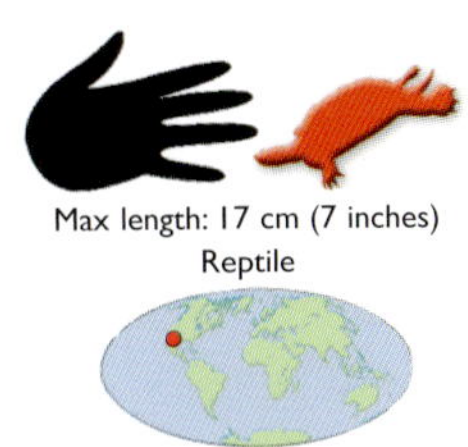

Yellow-blotched map turtle

The yellow-blotched map turtle is also known as the yellow-blotched sawback. This reptile grows to about 17 cm (7 inches) long, and is found only in the slow-moving rivers of Mississippi, United States, where it feeds on insects and shellfish. The yellow-blotched map turtle is endangered by the destruction of its habitat.

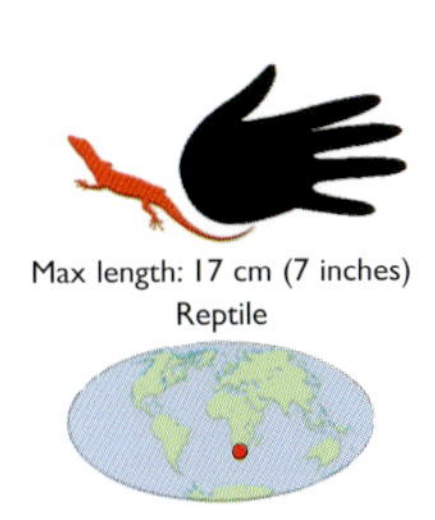

Zimbabwe girdled lizard

The Zimbabwe girdled lizard is a small reptile about 17 cm (7 inches) long. It lives in burrows beneath rocky ground. The lizard has a tail covered with backwards-pointing spiny scales. These scales make its tail look like an elongated pine cone. When threatened, this lizard runs into a crack in the rocks and raises its spines to stop it being pulled out.

Glossary

Amphibian An air-breathing, cold-blooded vertebrate that mostly lays jelly-covered eggs. Frogs, toads, newts and salamanders are the most common amphibians.

Amphisbaenian An unusual type of burrowing reptile that is often called a worm lizard.

Arboreal Describes an animal that climbs well and spends most of its time in trees.

Cacti A group of drought-resistant desert plants, most of which have spines instead of leaves.

Caecilian An unusual type of wormlike, burrowing amphibian.

Camouflage Shape, colour and pattern that help an animal blend in with its background, so that its enemies – and its prey – cannot see it easily.

Carapace The dome-shaped shell of tortoises and turtles. It is made up of overlapping scutes that are usually fused together into a solid dome.

Cold-blooded An animal that relies on the environment to maintain its body temperature. Fish, amphibians and reptiles are the main groups of cold-blooded vertebrates.

Constriction The method by which some snakes kill their prey. The snake coils tightly around its victim to prevent it from inflating its lungs and breathing. Death of prey is caused by suffocation.

Endangered Describes a species that has such a small remaining population that it is in danger of becoming extinct.

Estuary The lowest part of a river, where it enters the ocean. The water in an estuary is a mixture of fresh water and salty ocean water.

Fang A long, sharp tooth designed for seizing prey. A number of snakes have hollow fangs that inject venom when they bite their prey.

Freshwater The word used to describe the water from rainfall, rivers and most lakes. It does not contain salt.

Glossary

Gills Organs that extract oxygen from the water. Before metamorphosis, amphibians breathe through gills, although most develop lungs when they become adults.

Habitat The combination of landscape, climate, vegetation and animal life that forms the natural environment for a particular species.

Invertebrate An animal that does not have an internal skeleton with a backbone. Insects, snails, spiders, worms and millipedes are all invertebrates.

Juvenile An animal that is not full-grown.

Lungs The breathing organs (usually a pair) used by mammals, birds, reptiles and most amphibians.

Mammal A warm-blooded vertebrate animal that produces live-born young. Most mammals are covered with hair and live on land.

Marine Describes something that is associated with the seas and oceans.

Metamorphosis The process by which amphibians and many insects change from a juvenile body shape to an adult shape.

Oxygen The chemical gas in air, which is essential for living things. Land animals take oxygen directly from the air into their lungs. Animals with gills can extract oxygen from the surrounding water.

Polluted Describes environments and habitats that are affected by the presence of unnatural substances, such as chemicals from vehicle exhausts.

Glossary

Predator An animal that hunts and eats other animals.

Prey An animal that is hunted and eaten by others.

Reptile A cold-blooded, air-breathing, vertebrate animal that lays eggs mostly on land. Crocodiles, lizards, turtles, tortoises and snakes are all reptiles.

Ribs Part of the vertebrate skeleton – pairs of ribs curve around the major internal organs (such as the heart and the lungs), to protect them from injury.

Scales Small, disc-like plates that protect the skin of fish and reptiles. Reptile scales can be smooth or rough, and may be triangular in cross-section.

Scutes Large, bony scales that protect the skin of alligators, crocodiles, tortoises and turtles. The scales on a snake's head are also called scutes.

Shellfish A non-scientific term for invertebrate water creatures (such as crustaceans and most molluscs) that have a hard outer shell.

Species A particular scientific group to which an individual animal (or plant) belongs. Each species is a unique design for life and has a two-part scientific name. Members of the same species all share characteristics and differ only slightly in size or colouration.

Sub-species A group of animals belonging to the same species that share the same variation in their characteristic features. Some animals that are widely distributed have a number of regional sub-species.

Tadpole The juvenile life-stage of a frog or toad. Tadpoles are legless, live entirely in water and breathe through gills.

Temperate Regions that have warm summers and cool winters. They occur between the subtropics and the poles.

Glossary

Toxic Poisonous. A toxin is a poison produced inside the body of a living thing.

Tropical Regions around the Equator, between the Tropic of Cancer and the Tropic of Capricorn. A tropical climate is usually hot and rainy.

Venomous Capable of delivering a poisonous bite or sting. Venom is any poison produced by an animal for the purpose of injuring another animal.

Vertebrate An animal that has an internal skeleton arranged around a backbone. Fish, amphibians, reptiles, birds and mammals are all vertebrates.

Warm-blooded Adjective describing an animal that uses some of the energy it gets from food to maintain its body temperature at a constant level. Mammals and birds are warm-blooded.

Webbed Describes a hand or foot in which the individual fingers or toes are joined together by flaps of skin.